Don't Count Me Out

A volume in the series

The Culture and Politics of Health Care Work
Edited by Suzanne Gordon and Sioban Nelson

For a list of books in the series, visit our website at cornellpress.
cornell.edu.

Don't Count Me Out

A Baltimore Dope Fiend's Miraculous Recovery

Rafael Alvarez

ILR Press
an imprint of Cornell University Press
Ithaca and London

The depictions of drug use and gun violence in this book might be disturbing to some readers. Full names of people quoted have been used with permission. Initials and first names were used for those who could not be reached.

First published 2022 by Cornell University Press

Printed in the United States of America

Library of Congress Cataloging-in-Publication Data

Names: Alvarez, Rafael, 1958– author.
Title: Don't count me out : a Baltimore dope fiend's miraculous recovery / Rafael Alvarez.
Description: Ithaca : ILR Press, an imprint of Cornell University Press, 2022. | Series: The culture and politics of health care work
Identifiers: LCCN 2022006259 (print) | LCCN 2022006260 (ebook) | ISBN 9781501766350 (hardcover) | ISBN 9781501766374 (pdf) | ISBN 9781501766367 (epub)
Subjects: LCSH: White, Bruce M., 1959– | Drug addicts—Rehabilitation—Maryland—Baltimore—Biography. | Drug addiction.
Classification: LCC HV5805.W47 A3 2022 (print) | LCC HV5805.W47 (ebook) | DDC 362.29092 [B]—dc23/eng/20220512
LC record available at https://lccn.loc.gov/2022006259
LC ebook record available at https://lccn.loc.gov/2022006260

To the still-suffering addict

Contents

Foreword

If you read the first two chapters of this book, you will finish the whole thing. You know those roller coasters that shoot you out of the gate like a rocket so you can make the loop?

Imagine the loop being a continual circle of self-destruction, damage, danger, and an inability to stop harming yourself and everyone who loves you. That is the ride Bruce White was on for decades. And yet he stands sober today, a literal miracle.

Addiction is a black hole that sucks life, love, and opportunity into its pull. It twists and crushes everything until it gets you to the next drink or drug, and this goes on until you get sober or die. I read an article a few years ago that said one in seven people struggle with addiction. If you are one in which addiction takes hold, you simultaneously marvel at—and hate—people who can have "just a couple," as you continue to watch your life unravel.

The drugs and the drink are the symptoms, just a wicked way of medicating the addict's fear, rage, or both. Soon, they stop providing relief from the thinking, and physical craving takes over and puts you in a state where you will do all the things you swore you'd never do just to keep from getting sick.

Bruce White didn't come from extreme poverty but wasn't a trust-fund kid either. He was born into a solid, two-parent middle-class family who did the best they could to understand why their son—who was loved and had his needs met—became a fiend driven by drugs.

People who don't understand addiction say things like, "How could you do that to yourself?" "Don't you care about anything?" And my favorite: "You should just stop."

For an addict, it takes a bone-crushing moment—sometimes physical, sometimes mental or spiritual, or sometimes a combination of all three—to even consider getting sober. Everyone's pain threshold is different, and for the ones who never have that moment of "I will do anything to get sober," well . . . the ending is inevitably sad and tragic for all involved.

In this story, Rafael Alvarez gives us an unflinching look. It's as if you were right there watching, firsthand, in the presence of the beast. He writes with something that is lost these days: pure narrative, with no judgment. You, the reader, will decide how it affects you.

I am not a writer. I always had a daydream of being one but never developed the discipline it takes. Rafael is the real deal. He went to work for the *Baltimore Sun* as a teenager and spent twenty years on the city desk there. He worked on several TV and movie projects and was a staff writer, including for one of my all-time favorites, HBO's *The Wire*. So why would Alvarez ask a ham-and-egger like me to write this intro?

We have a mutual friend named Mick, and Mick introduced us, saying, "This is Ralphie, he's a dear friend." That was all he had to say, because I trust Mick in the old ways of the neighborhood. Mick is from Chicago, Ralphie is pure Baltimore, and I'm from Pittsburgh. If you're from those kinds of places and a guy you trust vouches for a guy, that's all you need. Our connection was fast, and I find Ralphie to be a good and very talented man. I was humbled that he asked me.

As I said, I am no writer and certainly no medical expert, so why let an overpaid clown write this? Because my name is Billy, and I am an alcoholic. While my addiction did not take me to the places that Bruce White's did, I caused enough damage for me to thankfully get sober. There was a time where I couldn't get through the day without a bottle of Jameson whiskey. Drugs were in my story, but for the most part I was what a friend called a "pure b-flat drunk."

A dozen years ago my wife was going to leave and take my then five-year-old son with her. I was about a hundred grand in debt and unemployable. Today, none of those things is true. My marriage is healed and healthy, my debts are paid up, I have an open and honest relationship with my son, whom I love more than anything. I am a worker among workers, and I have not had to drink for twelve years and counting.

A wise man once told me, "Billy, you can have a drink, or you can have everything else."

Reading Bruce's story is part of what you can do to treat your addiction. The story of a man who went further down the hole than you did, and made it back, serves as inspiration that it is possible to recover.

Another way the story serves a newly sober person is that it lets you know you don't have to go that far. Whether you are able to heed this or not depends on how desperate you are to get better. I hope that when you read this and know someone who is suffering, you will give them a copy. You just never know what ripple an act of compassion can create.

—Billy Gardell, actor / stand-up comedian,
Los Angeles, 2020

Don't Count Me Out

Introduction

ANYBODY CAN

I had written about badass criminals like Bruce White for decades—in the newspaper, on television, and in fiction under the morbid cloak of "The Monster That Ate the City of Baltimore." But until I met Bruce near the end of 2012, I never truly knew one.

White had been a notorious, gun-crazed biker/junkie and career criminal in a city with an entrenched heroin problem going back at least to the 1930s, a two-time inmate who passed a seven-year stretch without a single visitor other than his attorney.

Our relationship began late in the summer of 2012 with a long-distance call from Baltimore as I walked my daughter's dog in Hollywood.

"Rafael Alvarez?"

"Yes?"

"I'm Bruce White," said a gravelly, right-to-the-point voice on the other end. "I hear you're a writer."

Indeed: Writer-for-hire; no job too small.

The day that Bruce called I hadn't worked in television for about five years, since the one-hundred-day Writers Guild of America strike from Halloween 2007 to Valentine's Day 2008. I'd driven to LA from Baltimore to work on a screenplay with my daughter while taking network meetings in hopes of landing a script—any script—to prevent a lapse in my WGA health insurance.

Bruce found me through Michael Salconi, an actor from Baltimore's Little Italy who played a uniform cop named Santangelo on the HBO series *The Wire.* I wrote for the first three seasons of the show, a much-heralded drama praised for everything from the social arguments it posited (never put your faith in institutions) to the nuanced humanity of its bad guys, some of them very bad guys.

But not even on *The Wire* did bloody reprobates take netherworld journeys worthy of Dante and Bela Lugosi and come back to tell the tale.

"When I flat-lined and the old dude in the other world said, 'I read your book,' I knew he meant the book of my life," said Bruce, recounting a moment from his near-death experience after being shot by a SWAT team. "After that sunk in for a few years, I knew I needed to write that book and knew I didn't have the education or talent to do it."

I'm not sure about the talent (always a wild card), but Bruce is one of the more intelligent people I've met in a lifetime of befriending strangers. Had things been different in his early years—if he had not been molested as a young boy, if the tens of thousands of dollars his family spent on hospitals and lawyers had gone instead to summer camp, travel, and tuition—his life surely would have been otherwise.

The son of a successful decorative box salesman and an elementary school teacher, Bruce was born into an all-white, postwar suburb of lawyers, doctors, and businessmen. As a child, he took dance and etiquette lessons and had all of his needs—and most of his wants—met. White's rosy memories of this somewhat idyllic childhood are brief, ending abruptly when he was six or seven years old and sexually abused by older boys in the neighborhood, the foundational trauma of many an addiction. By the fourth grade, he was smoking cigarettes and drinking wine in the woods. Marijuana soon followed.

Pot is often called the gateway to hard narcotics. For Bruce, simply being alive opened the floodgates to anything that would let him forget who he was. By his mid-teens, White was shooting dope and soon robbing pharmacies. He once allowed a jail doctor to remove part of his salivary gland just for the pain meds that came with the surgery.

Now in his early sixties and drug free since 2003, he said, "I used every hustle out there to get one more—just one more hit."

White was paroled after serving seven years (twice escaping attempts by other inmates to kill him), and for a while, the prosecutor who convicted him kept a photograph on her desk of Bruce in a cap and gown, college diploma in hand. It was a reminder that while rehabilitation among hardened criminals is rare, anything is possible.

A decidedly nonreligious man, Bruce is adamant that almost everything he does is an attempt to serve the will of the God who brought him back from hell in this world and the edge of Gehenna in the next. Of the journey, he says, "I was an animal, and then I had a Saul conversion."

It is a conversion in which he became drug free behind bars, began advising the same courts that sent him to prison on how to deal with fellow addicts facing jail time, and started a drug treatment center with absolute insistence on abstinence.

No matter how much progress the multibillion-dollar treatment industry makes in understanding the science behind addiction— and what little progress they have made has been slow—the spiritual component of recovery is cited as crucial by virtually every addict with quality recovery.

Against the twenty-first-century opioid epidemic, the Bruce White story is a detailed portrait of the brutal intractability of addiction while supporting an equal, illogical truth: even the most depraved junkie can recover from the progressive, fatal disease.

Addiction in all its guises has thoroughly saturated American society, and thus there are overlapping audiences for this book. It is neither self-help manual, academic text, nor religious tract. Just the story of one man.

This is a piercing look into the psyche of the addict, beginning long before the first drink was taken, the first drug ingested. It courses through decades of criminal activity, practically inevitable in the world of hard drugs. It may provide insight, for treatment providers, policy makers, law enforcement, and the long-suffering families and friends of addicts. The most prized reader, however, would be the hopeless junkie craving one more—"one more hit," as White puts it—the person who can't fathom the possibility of a way out.

Bruce White *was* that person. And, for some time now, he has not been.

"If I can get clean and sober," he said, "anyone can."

1

The Most Interesting Book the Old Man Had Ever Read

"You promised me he would not end like this."
—*Mernie, Bruce's grandmother*

On January 7, 1998—watching a movie and ingesting narcotics the way someone else might enjoy a bowl of popcorn—Bruce White yet again faced cinematic, near-certain death.

Soon to be forty years old, Bruce was in his room at his parents' home in lily-white Lutherville, Baltimore County, Maryland. A convicted felon, he'd been using drugs every chance he had since elementary school.

At first, he felt extraordinary pain, lost consciousness, and embarked on an adventure worthy of Alice, except that White's Wonderland was an especially odious subdivision of hell.

Bruce was the complete give-me-what-I-want-and-get-out-of-my-way-or-I'll-fuck-you-up dope fiend. He had seen and caused a lot of pain and ugliness to anyone unlucky enough to cross his path in a life devoted to drugs, kicks, fast machines, women, and violence. On the face of it, not a unique story.

But very few have experienced the sojourn Bruce took while minding his own business and watching a war movie at his father's home on a winter's night. Or at least come back to tell the tale.

Bruce awoke from a narcotic drowse with pain in his hand, having passed out in his bedroom with a cigarette between his fingers. He lit another and glanced at the TV to pick up the thread of *Platoon*.

"It was the part where Willem Dafoe is going into the tunnel. I always liked this part," said Bruce, noting that at the time—thirty-eight years old and weary of the street game—he was "lost in my own tunnel of explosions."

He kept a safe in the room and went to it for Dilaudid—an opioid painkiller—laughing because he couldn't remember the last time he was able to watch a movie in one sitting. Kneeling to open the safe, he hoped there'd be some "good red pot" left to complement the Dilaudid. He found a needle and the pills but was out of reefer. Reaching into the pocket of a pair of pants, he found a dollar bill and folded into it eight tablets of the Dilaudid—"all that would fit into the syringe"—and looked around for something to crush the pills.

The amount, he said, "was maybe three times as much as anyone might use."

Using a glass by the bed, he crushed the Dilaudid inside the dollar bill, shook the powder into a spoon, and tapped the rolled-up bill to get every last speck of dope. Putting a dab on his tongue he pronounced it bitter, familiar, and pleasant.

The ritual had begun. In the bathroom, he ran water in the glass, used it to fill a hypodermic needle, and then squeezed the water

FIGURE 1
Bruce leaving. Photo by Jennifer Bishop.

from the needle to the spoon. The powdered Dilaudid—yellow—also went into the spoon. Holding a lighter below the spoon, he watched the concoction bubble as the powder melted to clear yellow liquid. Taking the filter of a stubbed-out cigarette, he put it on the tip of the needle to filter impurities and drew the liquid into the syringe.

Ready, steady, go.

"Looking for a vein, I slide my bathrobe up and look at my inner thigh. Tapping the air out of the needle I look at my feet. Pulling the belt out of the robe I wrap it around my thigh, find my target, and slide the needle under the skin," he said.

He wishes that he wasn't on methadone, which dulls the effect of the Dilaudid.

Oh, well.

"Pulling the plunger back I see blood flowing into the needle, and as I slam it forward I already feel better. I'm home."

At the time, Bruce White was a convicted felon, having served time for firing a gun at a drug companion who had stolen a rug from his parents' house. On this night, police rightly suspected him of having illegal weapons, like the Mini-14 semiautomatic carbine he cradled while watching *Platoon* high on Dilaudid. Customized by a local gun shop that asked no questions, it was equipped with two forty-round clips and a pistol grip that allowed it to be fired with one hand. Like a kid with a toy, Bruce played with it in bed, using the laser sight to zero in on different spots around the room. In a gym bag on the floor were more ammo clips and a bulletproof vest.

It was now two-thirty in the morning, and Bruce decided to turn in to make first call five hours later at the methadone clinic. It was difficult to urinate with so many narcotics in his system, so he sat down on the toilet to pee and nodded off.

Coming to, he flushed the toilet, locked and loaded the Mini-14, and set it beside him on the waterbed, aware, as always, that there were many who might get a notion to rob or get even with the ruthless motherfucker he had become. Soon, he was out again.

And then BANG! BANG! BANG!

The front door to the White family home had been broken down.

"I grabbed my gun and moved to the other side of the bed," said Bruce. "Gun cocked, I put my right leg on the floor and raised my head toward the noise."

Extreme pain in his abdomen was followed by the sensation of his left arm "exploding," the letters SWAT now clear to him on a shield. The bullet went in and out of his arm, hitting the closet door behind him, flame visible from the barrel of the gun that had fired at him.

("I'd been shot at many times," he'd say later, "but never hit.")

"My right leg folded under me, and I flipped back, my trusted Mini now over by the television, and I'm several feet from where I began. The room was filled with the smell of burnt gunpowder, and I could feel a warm, heavy flow of blood covering most of my body."

Standing high above White with an automatic rifle pointed at his head was the county SWAT team cop, to whom Bruce said, "You shot me."

And then asked for his lawyer.

Medics took over to save the life of a man who'd just pointed an automatic rifle at police officers. Bruce has always maintained that if the SWAT team had identified themselves as cops, he would not have been so stupid as to aim a gun at sharpshooters. The ambo crew slowed the bleeding, and as they put Bruce on a stretcher, a tranquil feeling came over him.

A female medic walking next to the stretcher told Bruce he probably wouldn't live long enough to make it to the shock trauma helicopter. Did he want to go by ambulance to a new trauma center at Sinai Hospital, nine miles away? Bruce said okay and began to experience a silky peace—no pain, no fear. He thought that the head of the medic walking with him was glowing with white light, and he told her that if this is dying, this is easy.

"Don't," she said.

And Bruce White flat-lined.

> "But as for the cowardly, the faithless, the detestable . . .
> as for murderers, the sexually immoral, sorcerers,
> idolaters, and all liars, their portion will be in the lake
> that burns with fire and sulfur, which is the second
> death."
>
> —*Book of Revelation*

No white light for Bruce. No tunnel leading to a better place.

"I was looking down into a dark pit and saw what seemed to be souls going into it. I felt energy coming from the pit, and I was afraid of it," he said. "In my spirit I understood that they would never make it out."

As he approached the edge of the pit, cat skeletons with cartoon heads walked toward him, staring. And he knew beyond thought that the life he had lived had brought him to this place, the chasm where he would spend eternity. Then . . .

POOF!

Gone again.

This time, he was below water, a realm vibrating "with many secrets."

"I was breathing and moving as if I were on land," he said. "It was an odd place—with gravestones laying around, some falling over and many in disrepair. The water was cool on my skin. I had the feeling that if I was not careful I might be here for a very long time." In the near distance, a lean young man materialized, someone Bruce had known nearly his entire life. He excitedly walked toward the person, mostly skeletal with seaweed growing in his rib cage. What little flesh the man had was floating away with the current.

"It was Greg Burke, my oldest friend in the world," he said, "a kid I'd met in the fourth grade and one of the smartest guys I ever knew. He never amounted to anything."

When Bruce said it was good to see him, Greg smiled.

Two years earlier, Bruce had hugged Greg's mother at Burke's funeral—dead from a drug deal gone wrong in Mexico. Bruce asked his old drug buddy what he was doing below the sea.

"He said it was where he had to be," said White. "That it was his job to be there until someone else came along to take his place."

But where was *there*?

"He said it was a hull of lost souls, and it was his job to make sure that no one left, and that because he was 'newly dead,' the other souls were afraid of him."

Old friend to old friend, Burke asked Bruce for a favor: Could he watch the entrance to the hull so he could leave for a bit? He said he'd been there ever since his murder and needed a break. In the best addict tradition, Burke added that it would just be for a little while, that he'd be right back.

"He promised," said Bruce, "and I knew he was lying."

Adios, Greg, hello to a gaggle of large-headed, flat-faced prostitutes trolling the parking lot at "a hideous 7-Eleven," said Bruce, noting that the store leaned to one side with neon signs that buzzed like a swarm of insects.

"I was sitting in my old money-green, '69 Dodge Super Bee at this convenience store from hell. The car's hood had a chrome blower shaped like a woman that reeked of burnt flesh. All around the parking lot were old cars with the same chrome blowers on their hoods shaped like women. Some of the cars also had several on the trunk."

The hookers were leaning into the windows of cars, making deals. One of them looked Bruce's way, and he tried not to catch her eye. The closer she came, he said, the more he noticed a "pungent odor" he could only describe as the scent of drugs and death.

She greeted Bruce: "Hi!"

He said hello, afraid and confused.

"I wanted it all to stop," he said, desperate to know where he'd landed. "But I knew that it wouldn't."

What *is* this place?

"This," she answered, "is where you wait."

"Wait for what?"

She didn't know, and Bruce, aware that the woman was as lost as he, asked why the other cars had multiple chrome figurines of women and his car had only one.

She fixed Bruce with her gaze and said, "Because you only killed one woman."

He is blanketed with a loneliness as old as his earliest memory, and ...

POOF!

Now he's in a village that looks like the days of knights errant, the kind of place, he said, that children read about in storybooks. He sees men riding horses and lanes of small shops. He walks around, and people stare. Through the window of a shop that trades in relics, Bruce fancies a piece of metal.

"It shined like nothing I've ever seen," he said. "When I asked the [merchant] what makes the objects shine like that he says, 'God was here once a long time ago and everything around Him became like this.'"

Bruce wanted a piece for himself, one that resembled an icon. "How much?" he asked.

"One page of your book."

"What book?"

"The book of one's life," said the man. "Everyone here has one."

Bruce told the man he'd just arrived and didn't have one. Where you lay your head this evening, the shopkeeper says, is where you will find your book.

And he did—a volume of twenty-two-carat gold with the story of his life etched into every page, a book Bruce found too painful to read. Holding it close to his chest, he wondered how it had all come to this. All the while knowing very well how it had.

As Bruce left the room, he saw that three boys—all blond and blue-eyed—were looking at him. "I asked if they were brothers," he said. "They smiled and chimed 'yes' in unison."

The siblings knew a lot about Bruce, and he knew nothing of them. They said it was their job to help him "get to the next place." He thanked them and told them about the book he'd found in his room. Smiling again, they told him to follow them. The brothers told Bruce he could "spend" the pages in his book but that when it came time to leave, he would need every page to move on. When he asked if that meant that he shouldn't use the pages, they said it didn't matter, advising, "You're going to be here a very long time."

And then the shorter of the three—one that Bruce thought was "cool"—spoke music to Bruce's ears: "We used all the pages of our books to get high."

"High on what?"

"Everything."

The boys invited Bruce to go horseback riding once night had fallen, promising that they would all go out and party. He went back to his room to wait; a dank room with a broken dresser and a bed that sank in the middle. A window looked out onto the road, and while waiting for his new friends, Bruce stared at passersby, paced around, and looked out again.

"I didn't see anyone I knew or wanted to know," he said. But he was anxious to get high. Finally, the brothers arrived with a horse in tow for him. They rode to the next town, which, said Bruce, "had a much darker feel to it."

When the brothers asked what he wanted to do, Bruce said, "I thought we came to party." They laughed and slapped him on the back like a long-lost friend. "It felt good," he said, "to be with my own kind."

When the quartet knocked on the door of a nearby house, they were greeted by a tall woman with blond hair who was happy to see them. The short, "cool" brother introduced him as "my man Bruce," the woman gave White a hug, and in they went. Bruce thought the atmosphere was like a brothel in an Old West western, with whores and johns lounging about. The short brother called him into a back room where, he explained, all of them could get high and laid for five pages of Bruce's book.

"I knew I was being used," said Bruce. "But I gave him the pages right away."

The crew spent the night smoking PCP. Before getting back to town ahead of the sun, the brothers told Bruce not to say anything about their adventure and, if asked, to say they had been protecting the town from thieves.

His response?

"Can we do it again tomorrow night?"

Sure, they said, as if doing him a favor.

The next day, Bruce went to the relics shop to buy the shimmering piece of metal. The brothers were also there, and Bruce asked the short one which object he liked best. The boy pointed to a picture frame, half of which vibrated with the luminous presence of God.

"It wasn't my first choice," said Bruce, "but I bought it."

That night's rendezvous was set for dusk. The brothers left, and Bruce went back to his room, placing the icon on the dresser so he could see it from the bed, enjoying, he said, "the energy it brought into the room. I felt safe because it had been in the presence of God." And then he pondered something that had never crossed his mind on Earth.

"If I ever would be in the presence of God, I wanted Him to touch me the way He had touched the metal frame."

All that afternoon, said Bruce, he thought about God and knew the Almighty was nowhere where this troubled soul from Baltimore had been dispatched.

The brothers arrived at sundown, and Bruce pretended he was glad to see them. They galloped off to a different town to get high, one that seemed more dangerous than the first. He followed the brothers into an alley, where they dismounted and knocked on the back door of a house. Inside, said Bruce, it sounded like people were speaking Chinese.

The door was answered by a small, smiling Asian man who let Bruce and the boys in. He took them to a room, where they sat down, and soon returned with a small leather pouch. Inside the pouch were bags of white powder, a spoon, and syringes.

"My heart began to pound, and I felt like I needed to defecate," said Bruce. "China White, that's what I'd been longing for. The man said it would cost six pages of my book."

Bruce ripped out a half-dozen of the golden pages and handed them over.

"I took the spoon, tippled some of the drug into it, added water, and stirred," he said, repeating the ritual in the underworld as surely as he did thousands of times in his mortal life. "I pulled some fuzz from my sock and put it on the needle as a filter, pulling the liquid into the syringe. I placed my wrist under the fold in my knee, found a vein in my arm, and shot up." Immediately, he said, he nodded into a haze of opiated dreams.

Bruce woke up the next morning in his room, his book empty of its remaining pages. They'd been stolen by the brothers. How, he wondered, could he get to whatever place was next without his book?

As he washed his face, his eyes kept drifting to the pageless book on the table. He never saw the brothers again.

Walking around the town, Bruce met a few people who were genuinely nice to him, which felt odd to a guy whose entire life had been transactional. A few told him that the thieving brothers had been in that place longer than anyone else, that it was their custom to trick others to keep them there as well.

What should I do? Bruce asked.

"One man told me to walk the catacombs. He pointed to the steps by an old church and said that wise men lived there."

Bruce went to the dimly lit and musty steps and walked to the bottom. A bit of sunshine made it to the bottom, which led to a passageway. On his left were many locked rooms; a cold, damp wall was on the right. The path curved to the right, and he followed it. Several of the rooms were behind iron bars, and through them Bruce saw books, many volumes of different shapes and sizes. He tried to open one of the gates for a better look but couldn't.

Turning another corner, he saw a light in the distance. Following it, he came upon a man sitting down and reading a book; a very old man with long white hair and a long gray beard. He wore an old, soiled robe.

"He looked up at me, barely giving me a second thought, and went back to his reading," said Bruce. "When I was next to him, I said 'Hi,' and he looked up with a smile and said 'Hello.'"

Bruce asked the man what he was doing, and he said he was watching the books—that was his job, to keep an eye on them. Bruce confessed that he had squandered his pages getting high with the brothers; said he was afraid he would be stuck there forever.

The man smiled and called him by name.

"Young Bruce, do not worry," he said. "I have been reading these books for a very long time. And yours is one of the most interesting. Stop worrying and go on."

With the old man's words, Bruce felt pain in his stomach and reached down to find fresh blood. Looking at his body, he saw a white cloth across his abdomen, with blood trailing onto his thighs. "I was on the dirt floor of a cell with iron bars and a straw mat," he said. "Someone was talking, and I strained to hear what they were saying."

It was the voice of his maternal grandmother, Mernie Johnson, dead for a dozen years. Bruce knew then that he was dead and knew that wherever he was, it wasn't paradise. Yet the sound of his grandmother's voice was great comfort. Mernie was pleading for the salvation of her grandson's soul to a Power whose response was beyond his hearing.

"In my soul, I heard her say, 'You promised me he would not end like this.' And in my soul I could feel the answer: 'That was when you were alive. . . . did I not keep My promise?'"

Mernie, Bruce said, "begged and begged, almost chanting, 'One more chance, one more chance . . . please give him one more chance.'"

To Bruce's right were a pail of water and a rag. A pair of feet appeared in front of him, and without looking up, he took the rag and began washing the feet.

"The next thing I knew," he said, "I was in a recovery room at the hospital, very much alive and in real pain. I wished I was dead."

As Bruce's spirit rushed back into his body, he returned to the cold, physical world of life on life's terms.

Resuscitated on the operating table, he felt the pain unbearable; the mortal veil returned between him and the world to come.

That book that made the old, bearded man in soiled robes smile? The one he said was among the most interesting he'd ever read?

Though but a shadow, this is it.

2

Birth / School

BEFORE IT GOT UGLY

"I'm not sure if I wouldn't listen or couldn't listen. Looking back, I wish I would have listened to everything my mother and father said. All they ever did was try to help me."

—*Bruce White*

Snow fell hard on Baltimore the day of Maxine White's baby shower, March 15, 1959. The weather was so severe that many guests could not attend. Those who did joked that it was an omen: Mother Nature was sending Maxine a hell-raiser.

Maxine laughed and opened presents: diapers, bottles, crib sheets, and several dresses for the girl she wanted after two boys.

A month later—at 5:40 p.m. on April 20—Bruce McDorman White was born, by all accounts a healthy, happy child, a beautiful boy—so said his mama. The child arrived on the last ripple of the baby boom, in the final years of the Eisenhower administration.

Thought to have been conceived during a "let's make up" interlude on vacation following a marital spat, Bruce was the third son and last child born to Charles White and the former Maxine Johnson. The Whites were somewhat older parents—Charles was forty-one, Maxine in her late thirties—in a solidly middle-class suburban home just north of Baltimore, a house of drama, discord, and drink at 33 East Seminary Avenue.

"Mom liked her gin and tonics, and she and Dad always enjoyed a drink when they got home from work. Some nights many drinks," said Bruce, who believes he inherited the disease of addiction before running with it to the edge of the grave.

Drinking in the White household was a daily, mostly controlled pastime, with neighbors regularly having cocktails in each other's home. The sedative Valium—introduced to the US market in 1963 and soon the most prescribed medication in the nation—helped Charles and Maxine take the edge off the rat race and the raising of three boys.

Bruce was born at Maryland General Hospital on the corner of Linden Avenue and Howard Street in downtown Baltimore weighing seven pounds, three ounces. His complexion was exceedingly pink, and his hair was blond, thick, and curly.

His father—Charles Wood White Sr. of Baltimore—was a cardboard packaging salesman for L. Gordon & Son, one of old Baltimore's many paper companies. Still in business, the Gordon firm made decorative boxes for retail products, including Milky Way candy bars, Whitman's Sampler, and, most famously, Ouija boards. Charles, who never finished high school, liked being on the road and making calls, answering to no one but himself as long as his numbers were good.

Maxine taught first grade in the far Southwest Baltimore neighborhood of Morrell Park, then a predominantly white, working-class community near the county line. After Bruce was born, she took a few years off from teaching to tend to her boys.

Maxine met Charles almost a decade after her fiancé was killed in World War II. She dated so seldom that her mother worried she

FIGURE 2
Bruce McDorman White baby photo, 1959. Source: Bruce White.

might never wed. Charles and Maxine were married at the Johnson family farm on Maryland's Eastern Shore. The groom was in his early thirties, Maxine about four years younger.

Their first child—Charles Jr., known as Woody—was born on September 16, 1946. The Whites' second son—James Anthony, called Andy, came along ten years later, on July 10. When Andy was born he was cross-eyed, and he would go through several operations to help fix his eye problem. Andy's eyes were never good; he was legally blind in his right eye and nearly so in the other.

Woody—Bruce's senior by a dozen years—wore glasses but could see much better than Andy. Bruce never needed glasses until he began to age.

On long trips, Andy would quietly look at books—often about cars and trucks—with a magnifying glass.

Woody was pretty much out of the house by the time Bruce went to first grade, and he no longer went on family vacations. Andy and Bruce did most everything together as kids—walking to school, taking dance lessons, and going to kiddie parties in clean shirts and new shoes.

Maxine's wish for a girl was soon forgotten when Bruce was born without the weak eyes of Woody or the severely crossed eyes of Andy. In Bruce's baby book, she describes his birth as "without complications." (There would be far more observations—no doubt less cheery—but the diaries Maxine kept did not survive her. "I put them all in the grave with her," said Woody. "I didn't even look at them.")

Bruce's parents enjoyed their cocktails each evening and many on the weekends and vacation. They played popular games of the time at the kitchen table: Yahtzee, Mahjong, Scrabble, and Chinese checkers. Sometimes they watched TV before they retired to separate bedrooms, ostensibly because of Charles's snoring.

They were very much the 1960s suburban American couple in Lutherville, about eight miles due north of the Baltimore city line.

By the time Bruce came along, the middle-aged Maxine and Charles lacked the inclination—or ability or willpower or perhaps the energy—to discipline their children. And they were woefully unprepared when Hurricane Bruce slammed into the polished veneer of their lives.

Bruce was a curious, intelligent, and hyperactive toddler with a rebellious streak that deepened as he grew.

After years of self-inflicted torture, he would come to see himself purely through the lens of addiction: self-centered in the extreme. This held true whether his safety or someone else's was at stake.

In Bruce's baby book, he is thusly described by Maxine:

> Talks constantly and doesn't take stuff from anyone.
> Rough and tumble, bites like the Dickens if he gets the chance.
> Knows right from wrong, looks at you while getting into something
>   else with his other hand.
> Whistles at 11 months, just walking alone.

When Bruce was fourteen months old he was baptized into the Episcopal faith in Kent County on Maryland's Eastern Shore. His mother's family had long owned land there, the sprawling Brice-Johnson Farm on Galena Sassafras Road near the small town of Golts, just south of Maryland Route 290. The June 26, 1960, ceremony included his infant first cousin Dana Lisa Johnson, daughter of Maxine's brother Anthony C. Johnson, known as Butch. It would be the only religious ritual in which Bruce would take part for the next fifty-five years.

The farm where Maxine grew up and learned to cook—several hundred acres of grain, vegetables, and cattle, family land going back to before the Civil War—played a big part in Bruce's childhood. The Whites often took the ninety-minute drive from Baltimore to spend weekends and long summer visits there.

"My great-grandmother was born on the farm at the end of the Civil War, they called her Rennie," said Bruce, who rode horses and shot rifles there as a boy. "They say she lived to be a hundred and two."

Rennie Reynolds and her husband, "Dad" Reynolds, lived in a small home in the northern Delaware town of Townsend, the area where Maxine and Charles are buried. Their daughter was, Marion "Mernie" Johnson, Bruce's maternal grandmother.

Much of the farm has since been sold off—in 2001 it was listed at 198 acres. In Bruce's youth, Mernie the matriarch prospered there along with Butch and his wife, the former Virginia Carmer, parents of Dana and her two sisters.

Mernie was the widow of Clayton Johnson. She liked Charles—they both enjoyed a good game of Chinese checkers—but Butch was not fond of his sister's family. As Bruce's drug use became more reckless, whatever feelings Butch had for his nephew sunk to nil.

When Butch died at the farm on October 26, 2016, at the age of eighty-four, neither Bruce nor his brothers received a call.

"I'll always have fond memories of my uncle, but he didn't much care for us," said Bruce after learning that the last of his mother's siblings had died. "I believe he had a decent relationship with my father, but my addiction destroyed any relationship we might have had. After a while that side of the family had zero to do with us."

An example: Over Christmas (Bruce believes it was 1986, when he was twenty-seven), the young junkie and his junkie girlfriend named Tracy went to the family farm to celebrate the holiday, as the Whites had done for decades.

"Tracy and I had been doing dope all day, and then we drove to the farm, extremely high," remembered Bruce. "Driving down the long lane toward the hunting lodge I would give her hints of what she could and couldn't do" in order not to offend. "She looked at me like I was an idiot."

After arriving, Bruce and Tracy did some more drugs with other guests their age out of sight of the "grown-ups"—reefer, coke, Valium—and about an hour later they sat down to a traditional Christmas dinner. As everyone opened presents after dinner, Uncle Butch asked Bruce if he could have a word, and the two of them spoke in the hallway. Butch was quite angry, telling Bruce he didn't want Tracy on the property ever again and it would be best if they left.

Later, Bruce's mother told him that Butch believed Tracy had stolen money from Mernie's purse on a recent visit to the Whites in Baltimore. "It was me that stole the money," said Bruce. "But I let my mother believe it was Tracy."

With a reasoning common to drug addicts, Bruce added, "I never meant to be an embarrassment to my family, but I always was."

Woody recalls spending good times with his uncle Butch, remembering that his mother's brother "cared a lot for me, I hung out with him all the time on the farm." He said that his uncle's decision to raze Mernie's nineteenth-century farmhouse—

complete with marble fireplaces—upset him greatly. But not as much as Bruce's behavior pissed off Butch.

In 2016, Woody sent his Eastern Shore cousins a Christmas card asking about his uncle and never heard back. By then, Butch Johnson had been dead for two months.

On the outside, life in the White family was typically all-American—white privilege amplified with new cars and private swim clubs as the 1960s moved from a prosperous, somewhat permissive society to one quickly becoming weird, violent, and unhinged.

Walks to and from the well-regarded public schools included a path by a stream that Bruce loved more than being in class. Birds in the air, fish in the water, critters in the woods.

Outwardly gregarious and deeply insecure, Bruce was a kid who would do just about anything to have a friend. He would eventually be put on medication to calm down but usually threw the pills away.

He made friends easily, with a hunger to know that someone else—often the oddballs and outsiders—liked him in return. And he never believed that he was likable enough.

Bruce walked to school with his brother Andy, not quite a mile from their front door. Until he was about ten, Bruce was Andy's tag-along. After that, Andy became the sidekick, as Bruce established himself as a rough kid who eagerly waded into the ocean breakers on vacation, while Andy was more comfortable near the shore. They would stop at a stream on the way to school and skip stones across the water. "I loved the way the stones flew across the water," said Bruce.

Once, when Bruce was fifteen and Andy was seventeen, someone was picking on Andy on the boardwalk in Ocean City, Maryland.

"The guy was making fun of the way Andy walked," Bruce said. "I hit the guy in the face as hard as I could as many times as I could until I missed and punched the bench the guy was on and broke my wrist. Then I started hitting him with my other hand."

Always acting up and rarely paying attention, Bruce would get excited by just about anything, sometimes to the point where he either didn't or couldn't hear what was being said to him. Unable to sit still, he often ran around until he dropped from exhaustion. He could not stay in bed even when he was sick, on the chance that he might be missing something.

His childhood was well provided for and often joyous. Bruce held his father's hand while jumping waves at the beach, laughing with glee; spied boats bobbing on the horizon with binoculars; ate sandwiches on the sand and washed them down with homemade lemonade.

His earliest memory?

Getting knocked out cold as a three-year-old for ignoring a grown-up's advice that leaping before you look is a dangerous way to go.

Maxine was hosting a lunch of snacks and cocktails for a few neighborhood women, several of whom brought their children along. Bored watching TV in the den with the other kids, Bruce began running up and down the basement steps, jumping from one of the risers to the floor.

Maxine told him to stop, that he might get hurt. Bruce said "okay" and went back to his shenanigans as soon as his mother was gone. One of the other kids reminded Bruce that he wasn't supposed to be jumping off the steps. Bruce pretended not to hear, jumped again, missed a step, and cracked his head on the concrete floor.

Out cold.

The boy who warned Bruce to quit fooling around began yelling, and all the ladies came running to the basement. The next-door neighbor, Ona "May" Miyamoto, got to Bruce first with a damp cloth that she gently pressed on his forehead. When he came to, it was her kindly face he saw.

"That's my earliest memory," said Bruce, who never let something as petty as a skinned knee or a measles shot upset him enough to cry.

It was a comfortable childhood with more than its share of Huck Finn—bringing snakes and turtles and frogs home to show Mom—interrupted by spurts of erratic and at times extreme behavior.

He rarely listened to instructions, was lost in his own world, and would disappear without notice—behavior that became more frequent and often public as Bruce got older. Complaints to the boy's father got Maxine nowhere.

"Forget it," Charles would tell his wife, mixing a couple of high-balls and settling in for a night of Scrabble before bed.

The week before Thanksgiving of 1963, Bruce's world, along with that of most everyone else, was riveted by the murder in Dallas of President John F. Kennedy. His mother and the other ladies in the neighborhood couldn't stop crying, and cartoons were yanked from television programming.

"Andy kept changing the channel," remembered Bruce. "And every station had news on."

In 1964, Bruce went off to kindergarten, at first upset that his mother would not be going with him before quickly enjoying being with other kids. He stopped missing home the moment he got on the swing set at recess, followed by cookies and milk and a nap.

Maxine was relieved to have Bruce out of the house for a few hours; she needed a break from him and hoped that school would provide some discipline. In the coming years, she would wish for that and much more.

There were plenty of birthday parties with lots of neighborhood kids in nice clothes and ice cream. Trips to the Baltimore Zoo in Druid Hill Park gave Bruce a glimpse of creatures that fascinated him—hippos and elephants, lions and tigers. But the animal experience that best tells the kind of kid Bruce was took place a few years later with his family's pet cat named Gray Ghost. When Bruce was in the fifth grade, Gray Ghost gave birth to a litter. This was an exciting event for Bruce, who told everyone in class about the kittens, especially one he named Jackson for a Native American character in the 1965 movie *Cat Ballou*.

The kid Bruce often walked home with in grade school was Robert Burn, who seemed keen on seeing the newborn kittens. Robert's mother—Helen Jean Burn (1926–2014)—wrote for Channel 67, Maryland Public Television.

"We always walked as far as the creek together and then went our separate ways home," said Bruce. "One day I thought Robert was going to come home with me and see the kittens. He said he didn't want to, that they were just kittens. I got very angry and shoved him in the creek. He slipped and fell and got wet head-to-toe. When he got out he said, 'I'll come see them tomorrow.'

"The next day I told him I was sorry," said Bruce, "but I don't think I was."

Years of false and self-serving apologies followed, along with escalating violence toward those who didn't do what Bruce wanted or somehow offended his twisted sense of propriety. By grade school, Bruce and his friends began drinking and smoking pot.

From fifth grade until the age of forty-four, when he got clean behind bars, Bruce's life would become steadily dominated by drugs and guns, violence, emergency rooms, and prisons. It appeared to dead-end with an eight-year stretch in the custody of the Maryland Department of Corrections.

Released from the maximum-security prison in Jessup in October 2005, Bruce would find early sobriety in Narcotics Anonymous but had—and still has—a lot of work to do to make peace with an extraordinarily ugly past.

It was while working the twelve steps of NA with a fellow addict that Bruce remembered and embraced an incident from early childhood, one of the very few he could conjure as an example that, at one time, he'd been "a kind and caring human being." It was the story of the horseshoe crab, and it was from that memory that Bruce began to rebuild his life.

Over the summer of 1964—when Bruce was five, Andy was seven, and sixteen-year-old Woody stayed home—the Whites went for a vacation in Rehoboth Beach, Delaware.

Maxine's sister Gwendolyn (1927–2015) was married to a man named John Hoch, who had built a cottage near the beach. The Hochs lived in Odessa, Delaware. Bruce had seen the ocean before, but this was the first time he truly remembered it. Bruce and Andy loved the beach, excited by the smell of salt in the air. To Bruce's young mind, there were way too many rules for having fun in the surf.

On one of his first afternoons by the water—in the heat of the day, the beach was less crowded—Bruce watched a man pull a horseshoe crab from the water, a creature he'd never seen before. He walked up and touched the pointy tail of an animal that evolved more than five hundred million years before Bruce saw the ocean. Bruce liked the way the crab felt to his touch, a hard, slow-moving thing more closely related to the spider than the crab. The man said they came close to shore to mate, which Bruce didn't understand. Then the grown-up returned the crab to the water, and Bruce ran back to tell his father what he'd seen.

What happened next prompted Bruce to remember on the far side of his addiction that there had been a time when he wasn't bad news, that he once possessed sane ways of thinking and behaving to which he might return.

Nearby on the beach, a couple of adolescent boys were pulling horseshoe crabs from the surf and flipping them onto their backs. They then filled the upside-down shell with sand, eight or ten crabs lined up, each being tortured to death by young sadists.

"I went over to them and didn't like it," said Bruce, who remembered putting one of the crabs back into the surf. "Then I went back and got another one and did the same thing."

The bigger of the two kids told Bruce that if he freed another crab he would beat him up. Bruce pointed to his father and his uncle nearby and said, "No, you won't."

The older boys walked away, and Bruce returned all the beached crabs to the surf as his father looked on proudly.

"By the time I began [practicing recovery] I was worried that I'd always been bad," said Bruce. "But in the horseshoe story something became clear to me. I remembered I wanted to do the right thing."

At about this same time—age five, the year Lyndon Johnson signed the Civil Rights Act and seventy-three million people witnessed the Beatles on the Ed Sullivan Show—Bruce experienced something that all the dope in the world couldn't make go away, something, he said years later, "I never wanted to tell anybody."

Sometime between the first and second grades, about a year or so after the day of the horseshoe crabs afternoon—the last time he remembered doing something without a selfish motive—Bruce was twice sexually molested by older boys. Once during a sleepover at a friend's house, and once by acquaintances of his brother Andy while at home.

"I was always a broken kid, always thought I was worthless," he said. "But this broke me in a new way."

The assaults were never far from the mind of the self-medicating ex-con out to prove to any motherfucker that he'd never be taken advantage of again.

Though he did not speak of the abuse for thirty years, all the dope in the world couldn't heal the wound.

3

Skipping Stones / Getting Stoned

GRADE SCHOOL

"Don't worry about it, Mrs. White, he'll grow out of it
as he matures."

— *Bruce's pediatrician*

When Bruce was a little kid, his family would drive to the Jersey shore in the summer where his father's brother and his wife—Uncle Jim and Aunt Joan—had a place near the beach. On the way, about a three-hour drive from Baltimore, Charles would stop a few times to squeeze in sales calls—the classic, middle-America 1960s hustle. When Bruce's father came out of whatever office he'd visited, Maxine could tell right away if it had gone well or not. Quite often, it had not.

After the second or third disappointment, Maxine would go into her purse and hand Charles a small, yellow Valium—five milligrams worth of tranquility. Whereupon Charles would thank her kindly, and the trip would proceed.

The next time Charles stopped to pitch a bucket of ice to an Eskimo, Bruce would read his father's face before Maxine did. "You better get a pill," he'd say. "Dad doesn't look happy."

The message was as clear as a sunny day at the beach: a pill could cure what ails you.

These were the years—from toddler through about the first grade—when Maxine described Bruce as a boy with an "easy nature," a spirited kid who got along well with other children; who loved nature and often brought home wounded animals (he once built a pond for a crippled turtle) to take care of.

A mother's pride and hopes are preserved in Bruce's baby book, one of the few remnants of his childhood to survive many moves, prison sentences, home robberies, and forgotten storage units.

Around the same time as the early family vacations he remembered, which rarely included Woody, Bruce came down with some kind of bug and ran a temperature well over a hundred degrees. He was hospitalized until the fever broke, and to pass the time, he received a GI Joe soldier from his father.

Bruce loved the toy—an eleven-and-a-half-inch "action figure" with twenty-one movable parts—the first American "doll" marketed to boys. During his stay, another boy was brought into his room with badly burned legs. It was said that the boy had been playing around an oven when he was injured.

"I tried to talk to him," said Bruce. "But he didn't want to talk."

The next day, feeling much better and less feverish, Bruce woke up to play with his GI Joe but couldn't find it. The kid in the other bed was playing with it, and when Bruce asked for it back, the boy said it was his. Bruce asked a nurse to get it for him, and the nurse did.

When Charles came to visit his son, Bruce told him the story. His father explained that the boy did not have a family like Bruce did.

"I felt sorry for him," said Bruce. "When I got out of the hospital, I let him keep the doll."

Bruce attended Hampton Elementary School—peanut butter and jelly for lunch with chips and two cookies packed dutifully by Mom—about three-quarters of a mile from his home.

FIGURE 3

Bruce, in Cub Scout uniform, with his first drug buddy, Greg Burke (*far right*). Source: Bruce White.

From the first grade on, teachers were telling Bruce to calm down—sit in your seat, stop talking, pay attention—and Maxine was asking the family physician what was wrong with a kid who seemed to live inside his head.

The wondrous part of Bruce's childhood took place in nature, in streams and culverts and miles of woods and trails near his suburban home. He played some organized sports—in baseball he was a catcher—but never cared enough to do the work it took to excel.

When Bruce's mother went back to work at the beginning of his second year of school, he and his brother Andy and other neighborhood kids walked to school together.

"There were two large tunnels directly under the road" near the stream, remembered Bruce. "One of them was a large round [concrete drainage] pipe, and you could crawl inside. It went on forever.

"I'd stop at the stream and skip a few stones across the water. I was good at it, and I liked showing off."

In a school play, Bruce portrayed a talking tree, a role he enjoyed because he got to stand onstage next to a girl he liked. In second grade, the gym teacher caught Bruce looking up her skirt. He remembers it as both thrilling (the looking) and humiliating (getting caught).

That same year, age seven, Bruce was bringing in *Playboy* photos he found in Woody's room and showing them to other boys on the playground. For Bruce, the best part of the nudie pix was the way the other boys laughed and enjoyed it, as though he had earned their admiration with the prank. So he started bringing in pictures of naked women as often as possible.

"All he needs is some direction," said his second-grade teacher, who promised Maxine she would keep a close eye on him, seating him in the middle row near the front of the class.

Direction, development, and discipline. Blah, blah, blah, for years to come.

Maxine had come to realize that it was easier taking care of other people's children as a first-grade teacher on the other side of town than summoning the energy it took to stay a half step ahead of Bruce.

From age seven to just about nine years old, Bruce and Andy attended formal dance and etiquette lessons at a local church on Friday evenings. They were taught to waltz, do the foxtrot, and if there was any time left over, could jump around to Beatles songs.

Bruce enjoyed the two hours of refinement—girls were there, girls he liked and who liked him—but hated when the boys at school teased him about it.

"I told them I hated it and had to go, but I kind of liked it," he said, noting the friends he made from other neighborhoods and a girl named Amy whom he began calling on the phone between lessons. For the comely Amy, Bruce bought a forty-nine-cent friendship ring at Kresge's five-and-dime.

"I asked her to take a walk behind the church before class started one night and told her I really liked her," said Bruce. Amy said that she liked him too, and he gave her the ring, for which she thanked him, then slipped in her pocket.

Bummer!

Bruce said nothing, and they went into the church for that week's lesson. Just before the last dance of the evening, Bruce noticed that Amy had put the ring on. Smiling, he took her by the hand and led her out to the floor.

From time to time, Charles and Maxine would find Bruce talking to himself. In school, his favorite subject was recess.

"I'd sit at my desk and daydream about going to the stream after school," he said. "Or I'd stare out the window and look at the playground. I was pretty good on the monkey bars."

Bruce's world, where he appeared hyper half the time, unresponsive the rest, was a happy place for the only person who resided there. One morning in the summer between first and second grade, Maxine took him to the doctor to see what might be done. Bruce was doing something in the basement, and she had to call him many times before they could leave the house.

Once at the doctor's office, he immediately began to touch all the medical equipment and was reprimanded before the doctor entered the examining room.

"He's a wonderful boy when he can stay focused," Maxine told the doctor, who reassured her that Bruce was in fine health and prescribed small green pills, most likely amphetamine, the kind of "greenies" favored by ballplayers in the 1960s. Bruce hated the pills and showed no improvement.

By the third grade, Bruce's obsession with motorcycles had taken hold, and he set his sights on getting a minibike, a big 1960s fad for boys. On the first day of school that year—as the students were called on one by one to say a little bit about themselves—Bruce enthused about the minibike he was going to get as soon as he earned the money.

"There were trails down by the stream, and I'd watch the other boys ride," said Bruce, who yearned to join them the way other boys dreamed of making a sports team.

Bruce mowed lawns to scrape up the money, and even though it wasn't enough, his father made sure he got a used, silver Rupp Roadster, a popular minibike with a pull-cord engine. Brochures for the bike—sold from 1968 to 1971—called it "a groovy way to commute to and from school."

As fourth grade began, Bruce considered himself groovy and becoming groovier by the day. This was accelerated upon meeting Greg Swafford Burke, a shy, awkward transfer student from Saint Paul's School for Boys, a nearby private school. The kid struck Bruce as strange and cool—"real, real skinny, with hair hanging over his ears."

When it was Greg's turn to introduce himself to the class, all he could muster were a few mumbled words about liking to play the guitar. That clinched it for Bruce, who seemed to have a built-in radar—which he fine-tuned in years to come—for broken vessels who didn't give a shit. People like himself.

"I knew just about every kid on the first day of school that year except Greg," said Bruce, who jealously guarded his friendships. "I said 'Hi' to him because he wasn't talking to anyone else."

Greg lived with his mother and grandmother and a few siblings on the wealthier side of Seminary Avenue, not far from the Whites. The friendship marked the beginning of Bruce's transformation from a hyperactive kid who disdained help from doctors and shrinks to a self-medicating troublemaker. The two boys immediately began to frequent the Burkes' liquor cabinet.

René Eibl, a friend from the neighborhood and school, was part of the clique of little delinquents forming around Bruce.

"Bruce always went further with everything we did," said Eibl, whose father—Frederick Eibl—was the maître d' at the Tail of the Fox supper club not far from the neighborhood. "There was no chilling Bruce out. We were all crazy, but it was never crazy enough for Bruce."

Said Bruce, "I'd fight just about anybody. I lost a lot, but I'd fight you."

In the fifth grade, the Whites took their son to see a psychiatrist at the Sheppard and Enoch Pratt Hospital, Baltimore's premier mental health facility, opened in 1891 and known nationwide as Sheppard Pratt. The shrink prescribed Ritalin, the brand name for methylphenidate, approved in 1955 for treating hyperactivity. Bruce didn't like it and gave the pills to Greg, who enjoyed them very much.

"Greg was so broken it was incredible. He had a brother with a brain injury and parents that were even older than mine. A whole broken setup, yet he was really, really smart. He would do whatever he wanted and never got caught."

On the playground that September, Greg was the first player Bruce picked to be on his dodgeball team. "I looked up and down the row and picked the new kid," said Bruce. "I said, 'I'll take the new kid.'"

The rebelliousness rooted in Bruce but not always acted upon was given license by Greg.

"When I told him I hated dance class, Greg said I should just refuse to go," said Bruce. "It kind of shocked me, because I'd never heard of a kid disobeying like that."

Bruce's friendship with Greg was fast and intense, beginning with Bruce spending the night at the Burke home and doing things kids dream of doing if only their parents would let them: stay up all night, eat all the ice cream they want, and watch horror movies. Bruce remembers wanting "to be Greg's friend forever." And he would—with many ups and downs—until forever came sooner for Greg than most.

In the fifth grade, Robert Burn—he of the kittens and the creek incident—transferred into Hampton Elementary, and the gang of mischievous misfits was fixed.

"Robert and I were in the same class, Greg was in another one," said Bruce. "Many days at recess the three of us would just stand by the fence and talk. I'd be jealous when I'd see Robert and Greg hanging out without me."

The bond that held Bruce and Greg close was not only a lust for drugs but a shared recklessness. There was no risk of one of them betraying the other because it wasn't long before betrayal—stealing drugs from each other, sleeping with the other guy's girlfriend—became part of the game.

"Greg was treacherous, and he was a big influence on me," said Bruce years after Greg was killed while haggling over a heroin deal in Mexico. "Robert would eat acid, but when we got into heavy barbiturates and opiates—once it got real deviant—he was gone. Robert only acted crazy. Me and Greg *were* crazy."

By the time the sixth grade began, Bruce was no longer hanging out with "the good kids" from the neighborhood; he was consumed instead with Greg and Robert and getting high and riding minibikes. "The kids I grew up with and knew my entire life I abandoned for Greg and Robert and drugs," he said.

At Greg's house, the grown-ups—his mother and grandmother—weren't paying much attention. The first night Bruce stayed over (after Maxine had ascertained that the Burkes were "a nice family") he found Greg sitting in a lounge chair picking his guitar. Greg looked up, said "Hey," and continued to play.

(As for Bruce's own rock dreams, "I took a few lessons, but when I couldn't play like Jimi Hendrix after three weeks, I didn't care and stopped," he said. He remembers laughing at the "corny" folk tunes his fourth-grade teacher played for the class on an acoustic guitar.)

The Burkes had a club basement with a ping-pong table, a TV built into the wall, a pool table, and Greg's setup for guitar and amplifier. At home, Greg was more talkative and less shy, not the odd kid he seemed to be at school. And no one checked on what the boys were doing in the basement.

Maxine was concerned when Bruce came home and told her that he and Greg made their own breakfast at the sleepover—or that the boys hadn't seen Greg's mother the whole weekend—but not enough to try and break up the friendship.

One weekend night, Greg went into the back of his basement and grabbed a bottle of brown liquid—bourbon—motioning for Bruce and another friend who was there to follow him into the backyard. Outside, they smoked cigarettes and passed the bottle.

"Horrible tasting," said Bruce of his first sip of booze. But he kept on taking his swig as it came by and found that after a while it wasn't so bad. In fact, he was feeling pretty good, though he didn't really enjoy it. Booze was never his thing.

"It was something to do," he said, something that got him out of himself.

What was better than getting drunk for the first time?

Telling the other kids about it in school the following Monday, to be the cool kid, to be liked even though he wasn't sure what the other kids thought of his escapades. Greg didn't appreciate the way Bruce bragged about the things they did together. Back in school, he was again quiet and aloof. Bruce went on and on, making sure that everyone knew what a blast they'd had over the weekend.

Later, he would show off when the school held a one-and-done drug-education class before school let out for the summer, correcting the teacher about exactly what was an amphetamine and what was a barbiturate, proud of his expertise.

"I hadn't done these drugs or even smoked pot at this point, but hanging around Robert and his brother's friends I learned a lot," said Bruce. "[The teacher] said that red Seconal was amphetamine, and I knew it was a barbiturate." (The heavy sedative would be immortalized by blues guitarist Johnny Winter in his 1973 song "Too Much Seconal.")

Concerned by Bruce's precocious knowledge of narcotics, the teacher called Maxine, who did nothing. And, said Bruce, "it was just a matter of time before I tried them all."

The near weekly routine of staying over one another's house—either in Greg's basement or backyard or the loft in Robert's garage—went on for the next few years. At the garage, the boys would watch Robert's older brother and his friends smoke pot and drink and, Bruce remembered, laughing, "talk about how cool they were."

The younger boys wanted in, and when the older kids were reluctant to include them, they set about finding some reefer on their own.

"We were just drinking and smoking cigarettes but had our sights set on pot," said Bruce. "Summer was approaching, and we became more reckless. We all had small motorcycles and would camp out and drink behind Loch Raven Reservoir, riding the fire trails."

Bruce began stealing booze from his father and replacing it with water. Sometimes Charles would mention it, and Bruce would lie about it.

"My father was growing weary of my relationship with Greg and Robert," said Bruce. "He noticed a dramatic change in my defiant behavior. I never listened to him anymore."

Just like with Maxine getting a call from a concerned teacher about her son's copious knowledge of illegal drugs, not much of anything was done about it.

"One weekend when we were sleeping over Robert's we found a pipe with a piece of tinfoil in the bowl and some type of dirt rock," said Bruce. "We asked Robert's brother James what it was, and he told us hashish and we couldn't have it." According to Bruce, James said, "If you find something on your own, I'll show you how to use it."

And off they went the next morning, headed for the part of Towson—the seat of Baltimore County a mile from Robert's house—where hippies congregated.

"My hair was long for those times, and we looked the part for 1972 in our bell-bottom jeans and T-shirts," remembered Bruce. "My mother and father had much less control of me, and I enjoyed the freedom."

At a "head shop" and underground bookstore called Book & Tape Worm—the suburban version of what Baltimore wannabes assumed was "happening" in San Francisco—they encountered a young man with long hair just hanging around. They asked him where they could get something to get high on. "The guy said if we gave him five bucks he'd get us some hash and we should wait around the corner near the Brotherhood of Man [drug] counseling center," said Bruce. At the time, the irony was lost on him.

Bruce, Greg, and Robert did as they were told—hanging out in the basement of the "Brotherhood" with other young people—until the long-haired dude came back and motioned them outside.

The stranger gave them a little block of something wrapped in aluminum foil—they inspected it, found it looked the same as the stuff James had told them was hash, and rushed back to the attic in the garage to try it out.

When James opened the foil, he told the boys they'd gotten ripped off in their very first drug deal: it was about three dollars' worth of hash, not five. But it was hashish nonetheless, sandy blond in color and known as "Lebanese," though no one knew its origin.

"He told us to get the smoke deep in our lungs and hold it in as long as we could," said Bruce. "And then he told us to have fun."

The boys sat in a circle on milk crates and started to burn the hashish in a small pipe with wooden stick matches. Robert hit it first and then Greg and then Bruce.

"I could see the fire going down into the bowl of the pipe and see the hashish turning bright red as if it were charcoal at a cookout," Bruce said, remembering that Robert coughed violently.

"Now it was my turn," he said. "I held the smoke in my lungs as long as I could and started coughing like the other guys. When I stopped, I said, 'Right on.'"

The pipe kept going around, said Bruce, "until the hashish was gone." And then they debated whether they were high or not, since none of them knew what to expect. Soon, there would be little, if anything, about drugs that Bruce did not know from personal experience.

"After that first time with hash it was a summer of smoking pot, getting drunk, and riding motorcycles on the fire trails," said Bruce. "That five-dollar piece of yellow hash would be the start of breaking all of our other friendships, destroying any dreams we had for any kind of [positive] future.

"It was fun when we'd go into the woods and get drunk and then go up to the store and steal pies and milk off of porches, just being high and running around like kids," he said. "But everything that came after that—pretty much all of the next thirty-five years—all of it fucking sucked."

4

Failing the Seventh Grade

"I knew I was cool and so would everyone else once
they got to know me."

—*Bruce White*

M iddle school, said Bruce, "kicked off my descent into drug
addiction. Dealing and doing drugs were the only curricu-
lum I followed."

In his first attempt at the seventh grade he lost his virginity to
a girl named Kim at a party where everyone was drinking and
smoking pot. By ninth grade, said Bruce, "I was a dope fiend."

The journey from troublemaker to junkie included two years in
the seventh grade and many visits to the medicine cabinet of Greg
Burke's grandmother, the same woman who accompanied the ado-
lescents to RFK Stadium in Washington to see the Rolling Stones
in 1972.

"It was the Fourth of July," remembered Bruce of perhaps the
most fabled of all the Stones' tours. Mick Taylor was still on lead
guitar, and Stevie Wonder opened for the World's Greatest Rock
and Roll Band.

Another kid was supposed to go but couldn't make it, so Greg
invited Bruce. The boys were chaperoned by Greg's mother,

Nevada, and her mother. "The Burkes were pretty much hillbillies from Tennessee who wound up on the good side of Seminary Avenue," said Bruce of the suburban neighborhood he terrorized for decades.

"There was a guy sitting behind us smoking black hash, and he got me and Greg high," said Bruce. "Greg's grandmother was chugging a jug of wine and got her picture in the *Washington Post*. The caption said something like, 'the oldest person at the Stones' concert.'" Which doesn't quite mean the same thing as it used to.

"Greg had been using his grandmother's pills the summer before seventh grade, mostly barbiturates," said Bruce. "My family's medicine chest had my mother's strong diet pills."

With that arsenal in place, Bruce said he "was excited about going to Towsontown Junior High." By this time, he'd been getting drunk and smoking pot regularly but had never ridden a school bus.

"My mother took me to shop for clothes at the Merry-Go-Round in Towson. I'd picked out some really nice duds, all very expensive," said Bruce. "She liked me to look good and never said a word about the cost."

The clothes were cheaply made, early seventies post-hippie stuff from a store that had cornered the market on clothes for kids who wanted to look cool but were too young to run off to Haight-Ashbury (where by which time the scene had largely dissipated): lots of patterns, lots of colors, platform shoes worthy of Keith Moon, and pastel shirts with French cuffs.

"The bell-bottoms ran the gamut from low-cut ones to the elephant bottoms with the high waist. It made me feel better to have the nicest clothes in class, and I usually did. I went to bed that night very excited about the bus ride to school."

Before leaving the house for the first day of junior high, Bruce checked himself in the mirror and "smiled at my appearance, grabbed my lunch, and went to meet the bus." He immediately went to the far back—where else would a cool kid sit?—and claimed a seat that would be his for the next few years.

At the junior high campus not far from downtown Towson, Bruce saw fields of baseball diamonds and track and field ovals and dozens of buses letting kids off from many neighborhoods. "I knew that this was going to be a very different experience than elementary school," said Bruce, whose previous behavioral problems were more or less limited to BB guns and cherry bombs. "I had no idea there would be this many people coming to the same school."

Getting off the bus, Bruce noticed for the first time an African American man directing pedestrian traffic and the bus drivers. The man was J. T. Cunningham, and he also served as the cafeteria monitor.

"J.T. was the brunt of many of our jokes," said Bruce.

Perhaps, but Cunningham had the demeanor of a drill sergeant and a good nose for bad eggs like Bruce White.

"He knew we were punks long before we knew it. Every day when the bus arrived he'd say, 'Are we going to have trouble today, Mr. White?'"

Usually there was, as if stirring up trouble was the only reason to go to school. A classmate named Sid, a year older than Bruce, was often at the center of it. "Sid pointed out the cool kids to me," said Bruce. "That meant they smoked pot and ate pills like we did." (Much later, White would reflect, "The only thing Sid and I ever did together was drugs. But we stayed friends for years.")

In class, Bruce was grouped with the average students and worked his way down from there.

Bruce's first foray into selling drugs took place in the seventh grade, and it was as meaningful to him as making the school baseball team would be to someone else. His rookie experience selling small amounts of hashish immediately led to violence and the police.

An older teenager he met at a shopping center said he would "front" Bruce a quarter-pound of hash divided into small amounts, worth about $300 in the mid-1970s. The practice of putting dope on consignment—an act of trust called "fronting"—was one that the thirteen-year-old Bruce was not familiar with.

"A day or two later the guy came to my house, and we went into the garage attic where he showed me a large bag filled with rolled-up tinfoil balls of black hash," said Bruce. "He said it was a quarter pound broken down into grams." When the older kid left, Bruce dumped all the hash onto his bed and sampled the product. "It was very strong," he said, "and I loved it."

What Bruce loved just as much as a heavy buzz was crossing the threshold into the life of a celebrated drug dealer, a vocation that he would follow with tragic results—mostly for other people—over the next three decades.

"I knew I would be much cooler now," he said, recalling how he sold the tiny balls of hash at school for five and ten bucks each. "It would make me somebody."

Such self-esteem, say therapists working in addiction, only comes from peers who already support what you're doing. In Bruce's orbit, these would be his running buddies—all minors—who not only believed illegal drug use was acceptable but promoted it.

"At that age you are always concerned with what your peers think of you," said Robert K. White (no relation), director of behavioral health at the University of Maryland School of Medicine's

Department of Psychiatry. "You need a reference group, usually the outsiders, who think doing drugs is cool," said Rob White. "You would be shunned by certain groups but celebrated in another."

Bruce loved being feted by druggies. He got up the next morning, stuffed the pockets of his bell-bottoms with hash, and ran to the bus stop, where Sid met him with a bottle of booze. They smoked a few bowls of hash and chased it with the liquor while waiting for the bus.

At school, said Bruce, he and Sid "went behind the gym where all the cool guys hung out" and announced that black hash was available at five bucks a pop. Some of the kids bought on the spot, some said they'd bring money the next day, and one youngster ratted.

On the way to be questioned by the assistant principal— longtime Baltimore County educator Richard W. "Dick" Letsch, now in his late eighties and long retired—Bruce gave his supply of hash to a friend named Mike, a boy he would soon betray as dope became more important than friendship.

"Lots of things are vivid to me from my years of dealing with young people, especially those who were troublesome," said Letsch, who had no trouble remembering Bruce White and was not surprised to read about his former pupil's troubles in the news.

A few years down the road, as Bruce's addiction deepened, friendship only counted for so much. The same Mike who safeguarded Bruce's hash gave Bruce $500 for a quarter ounce of cocaine. Bruce—in need of a fix himself and afraid he was going to get sick—used the money to buy heroin, lying to Mike that the coke dealer had cheated him out of the money. "He knew it was a lie, and it looked like he was going to cry," said Bruce. "He left, and I never saw him again."

But back in the seventh grade, Mike was loyal enough to hold his friend's hash as Bruce went off to see Mr. Letsch.

"He asked me if I was selling drugs, and I said no," said Bruce. "Then he opened his desk drawer and pulled out a foil of the hash I was selling. He asked me if I'd seen it before. I said no."

Letsch then asked Bruce if he had given hash to someone to be paid later. "Right then I knew who snitched on me," he said, standing by his denials while authorities searched his locker and called his parents.

My parents "didn't do anything about it," said Bruce, who that night consulted Sid about how to handle the situation. Sid said he'd give the hash and whatever money Bruce had collected back to their supplier, adding that Bruce had to "take care" of the snitch.

Claiming that he was a kid who operated on "fear and mistrust"— "I didn't trust anybody, and I feared everybody"—Bruce had no trouble giving the boy who had squealed an ass-kicking.

"Sid told me that if I didn't beat the kid up I'd be uncool," said Bruce. "I had fought my way through elementary school. If I put the look or the move on you and you bought that bullshit, I knew you were scared and came right in. But if you stepped up you might see the coward in me. After a while that went away too, and I'd just pop you in the mouth."

Bruce met Sid at the bus stop the next morning, they smoked hash, and off they went. All through homeroom, Bruce obsessed about beating up the kid who ratted him out, "the only one I had fronted the hash to, the one kid I didn't know very well."

"I was lazy," said Bruce. "But when I wanted something, I could focus."

After lunch, he saw the kid walking to art class, handed Sid his books (which he almost never opened), "and saw fear on the face of the kid as I walked toward him."

Bruce got the first punch in, "square in the mouth. He dropped his books, and it was on. Everybody was watching, and I pounded him with my hands and feet. I got suspended for three days. Nothing happened to the other guy."

Returning to school after the suspension, Bruce walked a little taller. "A lot of kids treated me like I was special, and I liked it," he said. "When they asked me what my parents did to me for getting in trouble, I told the truth: 'Nothing.'"

It's a trusted adage in recovery that "if nothing changes, nothing changes," and the rest of that year followed form.

"I would go to school stoned and clown around in class; it was to socialize, not learn," he said. "Many days I just wouldn't go at all, going into the woods to get high or walking around the shopping centers."

His report cards reflected as much, and his parents—while not pleased—didn't take any measures to find out what was wrong with their intelligent, wayward son.

Looking back, Bruce described his parents' response to his behavior as "sheer and utter confusion. They were sad and baffled at how fucked up I was and didn't know how to get me out of it." At the same time, he said, Charles and Maxine "had their own demons, lots of booze and pills."

Bruce didn't expect to fail the seventh grade—"it was humiliating"—but concedes that he did nothing to prevent it. That summer, his parents hired a tutor to help him, though the ability to grasp and retain knowledge was not the cause of his academic problems. The experiences that Bruce craved—physically, mentally, and spiritually—lay behind his failures.

"Shame began to run my life," he said, although the people who had to deal with him—both kids and adults—could not see it beyond White's facade of bravado and intoxication.

Being kept behind while most everyone else in his class moved on to the eighth grade was a disgrace, and Bruce determined to take his education more seriously. It didn't happen.

"The intent was there, but there was no change in behavior," said Bruce. "I'm not sure I had the ability to change at that point." That summer, he said, "was like all the others since I started using drugs." The family went on vacation to Ocean City, and Bruce brought drugs to be sure "it would be fun."

"My mother and father let me drink Ripple wine, and I remember passing out on the porch of our condo in a lounge chair. My father woke me, laughing, the next morning, and I was sick from the wine. He found it amusing. I was thirteen years old.

"My drug and alcohol use and ugly behavior was never a topic of conversation," he said. "The atmosphere in my house was that everybody got drunk. I'd come home late and stumble to my room reeking of booze and pot, and all I got were grim looks of disappointment."

More than a decade into his recovery, Bruce would observe that while he did more than his share of drinking, "I never really liked it. I couldn't function on alcohol." He claims that he conducted himself "at a very high level" on opiates and that "heroin fit my being."

When September of 1972 arrived, it was time to repeat the seventh grade. "I was taking too many pills, smoking too much pot, and drinking too much. I was stealing money out of my father's wallet several times a week: a twenty here and a twenty there. Sometimes a fifty.

"He'd catch me red-handed and never say a word," remembered Bruce. "I was out of control."

During his second waltz through the seventh grade, Bruce added LSD to the mix.

"One morning I was walking down the hall, and Sid walked up to me. 'Stick out your tongue,' he said. I did, and he put a tiny, square piece of paper on it. He told me to swallow it and have a nice day."

When the bell rang for class, shapes began to shift before Bruce. He began to giggle, feeling odd. He was tripping.

"There was no fear, I was just enjoying it," he said. "Sid was coming toward me from the other end of the hall, smiling and moving his hands in front of my eyes. It looked like his fingers were wrapped around my head."

Bruce would go on to take LSD more than two hundred times, he estimates. "I would take LSD with my friends and go to movies like Led Zeppelin's *The Song Remains the Same.*"

Shortly after LSD came PCP—a "dissociative" known as "angel dust" and "flakes." A favorite of biker gangs, phencyclidine was introduced in the 1950s as an anesthetic and taken off the market in 1965 because of hallucinogenic side effects.

And then Bruce began enjoying DMT, a psychedelic compound of the tryptamine family. A common effect of DMT is hallucinations of humanoid beings known as "machine elves." Bruce did not remember seeing these "fractal elves," recalling the spacey waves of sound as color and color as sound.

"PCP had some very auditory hallucinations for me," he said. "My LSD trips were good and bad."

He passed the seventh grade, but just barely, with the credit going to the tutor. All Bruce really cared for was narcotics, fast cars, motorcycles, and whatever girl he could persuade to sleep with him. But mostly drugs.

"That was my true ambition," he said.

By the beginning of the eighth grade, Bruce had tried "every drug I knew about except cocaine and heroin. I told myself that

I would never do those drugs because I didn't want to be a junkie, but I already was doing anything that made me feel better."

Whatever it took to not think about the fact that he was Bruce White.

"I would go out to the steps behind the building in the morning and smoke pot and get drunk. That was the entire eighth grade," said Bruce. "I learned nothing in class."

Learning nothing. Low self-esteem. Future dim.

The summer before the ninth grade, Bruce "met some guys who always had pharmaceuticals, and they became my new friends," he said. "I started eating way too many pills, and my parents could see the changes. Even I knew I was doing too much."

Bruce surmised that the ninth grade "was important" and determined to do better in school.

"It was high school," he said. "I'd have to learn something so I could make a living. My mother wanted me to be a doctor. Sometimes I wanted to be a professional baseball player, but I had no athletic ability, and I knew it."

Bruce was going to buckle down and pay attention, although he was still taking barbiturates daily. "During school I'd curb my use and try to stay focused," he said. "On the weekends I would get out of hand."

One night, a friend showed up with about one hundred pills that his brother had stolen from a pharmacy, a mixture of the barbiturates Seconal, Tuinal, and Nembutal.

"I bought them with the plan to make money, but that wasn't going to happen. For seven or eight days in a row I went to school intoxicated and needed help many times from other students just to get in or out of class."

In the first month of the ninth grade Bruce was sent to the principal's office for suspicion of distributing barbiturates in school.

While waiting, Bruce overheard school officials say they were calling the police.

Bruce promptly left. On the way out, he met a kid who asked him if he wanted to get high, and the pair left the school grounds together.

"We got some alcohol and started drinking, smoking pot, and taking more pills," said Bruce. "About 8:30 p.m., my friend's brother drove me home. This time I could see that my parents knew I had a real problem. They just told me to go to bed, and I said goodnight."

And that was the end of public education for Bruce White.

Next stop: the mental hospital.

5

Ninth Grade in the Psych Ward
(UNTIL THEY THREW HIM OUT)

> "Psychiatrists kept telling my parents, 'This kid is broken.' But really, I was a fourteen-year-old with a barbiturate problem."
>
> —*Bruce White*

One morning in late September 1974—Bruce's first weeks of ninth grade at Towsontown Junior High—Woody came into his brother's bedroom and told him, without pleasantry, to wake up.

"Mom and Dad want to talk to you."

"About what?" asked Bruce.

"What happened in school yesterday," answered his older brother.

Bruce rolled over to face the wall and said he'd be down in a minute. What does an addict do when he's up against the wall?

"I got up and opened my top bureau drawer and pulled out the baggie of barbiturates" that he'd taken to school the previous day, a mix of Nembutal and Anabarbital. "I took a couple of the pills, shoved the rest in my pocket, and got dressed."

Woody, Bruce's parents, and a friend of Woody's were waiting in the den. Andy was in the kitchen, eating breakfast. Before Bruce

FIGURE 5
Bruce's parents—Charles and Maxine—poolside, Ocean City, Maryland. "I realized they were really going to leave me [in the psych ward] when we were in the lobby," said Bruce. "How dare they?" Source: Bruce White.

could begin tossing his bullshit around, his father told him he was going to see a doctor.

To which Bruce responded with an addict's favorite inquiry of deflection: "Why?"

And his parents—trying to keep their son alive—replied, "Drug addiction."

"I don't know if I even thought there was something wrong with me," remembered Bruce. "I'm sure I thought there was something wrong with everybody else, given the circumstances."

Just five or six years before, Bruce had been a kid who couldn't fathom the idea of refusing to go to dance class. Still not old enough to drive, he'd now been using a wide range of drugs—just about everything available to a suburban white kid but IV narcotics—for several years.

He wasn't given time to pack a bag, much less a toothbrush, before he got into the family car with his parents—a 1969 Delta 88 Oldsmobile convertible, Palomino gold—for the five-mile ride to Sheppard Pratt. Woody sat in the backseat with him.

Bruce told his parents that whatever they were worried about was no big deal, that he was just doing the same things his friends did. As they drove in silence past the hospital's iconic gatehouse (placed on the National Register of Historic Places a few years earlier), Bruce saw a sign that said "Admissions." The message did not make an impression.

When they parked, Woody took a small suitcase from the trunk, and Bruce realized—through the gathering haze of the downers he'd taken about an hour before—that he wasn't going to leave with his family. When he attempted a wobbly escape, his father and Woody grabbed him and ushered him inside.

"They were done with me at school, and now I was here," remembered Bruce. "I realized they were really going to leave me when we were in the lobby, and it felt like punishment. How dare they?"

Bruce was taken into a small, locked room with a table and two chairs. A doctor came in and told the boy he was going to be evaluated. Bruce was compliant, not really caring, and adequately tranquilized by the pills.

And then Bruce began to do something unusual. He told the doctor the truth about his drug use.

"I'm sure I didn't give a fuck," said Bruce. "What were they gonna do to me? When I realized there was really nothing anyone could do to make me change was the point when I left society."

The White family left Bruce behind for detoxification and addiction treatment as it was understood in the early 1970s. "They left, and I was defiant," said Bruce. "No tears, no begging to go home."

He was shown his room and introduced to his roommate, a young man with long blond hair who had tried to kill himself. The guy had never met an addict as young as Bruce, and Bruce had never met anyone so young who had tried to kill himself.

Bruce lay down on his bed and passed out. Hours later he was woken by his roommate, who said it was time for dinner. After dinner, they hung out in the TV room, and later that night a nurse at the medicine window gave him two Nembutal.

"I institutionalize very fast," said Bruce, who would get to practice that skill often in the years to come. "I was Eddie Haskell saying, 'Good morning, Mrs. Cleaver,'"—referencing the *Leave It to Beaver* TV show of his youth—"and then I'd do everything I could to derail the system."

After breakfast the next morning, two more Nembutal. And another stop at the meds window after lunch. "They were giving me enough drugs to stay high," said Bruce, "so I did not mind being there."

Why would he?

Good food, pharmaceutical dope, and TV! Paradise at $147 a day!

"My parents told me how much it had cost for me to live at Sheppard Pratt, and I've never forgotten it," said Bruce, noting the figure represented 1974 dollars. "It was the only intervention they ever tried with me."

Back in his room, Bruce drifted off to sleep until the bell rang for dinner, for which he was provided an escort.

The Addict and the Nymphomaniac

Watching TV that night, Bruce met a girl a few years older than himself named Patsy, a seventeen-year-old committed to Sheppard Pratt by her parents.

When Bruce asked why, she said, "Because I'm a nymphomaniac." When Bruce asked what a nymphomaniac was, Patsy told him and soon showed him.

At dinner, Bruce asked, "How did your family know you loved sex?"

And Patsy said, "They caught me having sex in my bedroom, and then they caught me with a bunch of boys at once."

In reply, Bruce extended Patsy an invitation to meet him in the closet of the reading room. She accepted. That night, Bruce's Nembutal was cut back to one pill. He slept for an hour, woke up, and went back to the TV room, where Patsy was waiting.

"As soon as our eyes met, she got up and went into the reading room. I followed her," said Bruce.

In the closet—crowded with board games and books and other odds and ends—Patsy knelt down, undid Bruce's belt and pants, and began kissing his testicles. "I'd never had my balls kissed before," he said. "I'd had sex with a girl in the seventh grade, but I'd never had a blow job. It was wonderful."

And that was the extent of his psych ward love affair.

Once Bruce completed detoxification, he was moved into an adolescent unit, where he concentrated on his ping-pong game.

("I'm still a ping-pong-playing motherfucker," he said with bravado typical of his competitive nature. "If I care about something, I need to be the best.")

On the unit, he befriended a kid from Silver Spring named Chris, a fellow addict among the manic-depressives and schizophrenics. "Chris was as severely fucked up as me," said Bruce. "We played a lot of ping-pong and pool over the next couple of months. My guess is he's dead."

And if Chris happens to be alive, it is likely his guess is that Bruce is dead as well.

Ping-pong and shooting pool and how to get high in the nuthouse were Bruce's primary concerns. Once in a while a patient on a weekend pass would bring back some pot. He remembers once tripping on LSD while there.

"I would go to group counseling and say nothing. I saw a psychiatrist twice a week for forty-five minutes in absolute silence."

His assessment recommended a two-year stay at the hospital.

Every few weekends or so there would be a dance for the adolescent patients. Despite his childhood training in the foxtrot, Bruce seldom danced, fearing what others might think of him.

Before one of the weekend cavorts, he hatched a plan via telephone to escape with the help of friends on the outside. This is how the Great Escape worked: At 9 p.m., his buddies would drive up to the building where the dances were held. Bruce would run out and jump in the car, and the knuckleheads would speed away with their freed hostage.

But because Bruce was such a hard-headed and devious pain in the ass, he remained on staff escort whenever he left his room. At 9 p.m., his friends' car was waiting outside, but someone had snitched, and the hospital staff were interrogating the getaway driver by the time Bruce got to the door.

"I heard burning rubber and could smell smoke, which eventually filled the dance hall," said Bruce. "My friend had obnoxiously revved his engine and peeled away."

Merry Morphine Christmas

As Christmas and the new year of 1975 approached, most of the patients were making plans to go home for a day or two, the length of their pass dependent on how trustworthy they were. Bruce was given twelve hours to be with his family.

Roasting chestnuts, exchanging gifts, and singing carols were not on his mind. "I wanted to go home, get high, and bring drugs back [to the hospital]," he said.

On Christmas Day, Charles and Maxine drove to Sheppard Pratt to pick up their son. They had breakfast at the Towson Diner, not far from the junior high where Bruce last attended school, and went home.

"I went to my bedroom and looked in all of my old stash spots for drugs but didn't find anything, so I started calling some friends," said Bruce. One was John "Scott" Pettingill, a Seminary Avenue neighbor who had just gotten his driver's license.

Scott said he'd be over about 6:30 with whatever he could get his hands on and arrived in his family's Ford LTD Country Squire station wagon, a forty-eight-hundred-pound rocket with a 350-cubic-inch V-8 engine and 163 horsepower—a nineteen-foot-long rectangle of chrome and steel capable of hitting 100 miles per hour.

Bruce, of course, rode shotgun. The first stop was the house of Jerry Watson, a Catholic school kid who later took his life. Jerry and another kid jumped into the backseat. Then it was off to pick up one more guy, smoke reefer, listen to music, and laugh. Scott had brought Bruce half an ounce of marijuana and a few hits of LSD.

"The guys caught me up on everything I had missed," said Bruce. "It seemed like nothing had changed at all."

More pot, more laughs, and soon it was time for Bruce to get back to Sheppard Pratt, telling Scott, "I need to go home." Scott said okay and heeded the request with the same amount of respect Bruce afforded others: none.

"When we reached the stop sign at Seminary and Providence roads, Scott made a U-turn and headed back down Seminary Avenue," said Bruce. "He floored the accelerator, and the big engine kicked in. We were hurtling down a steep hill at 100 miles per hour."

And the tough guy riding shotgun was afraid. "I begged him to stop and let me out, I literally begged him: 'Please Scott, slow down, you'll never make the turn.'" But Scott, he said, "had a faraway look in his eyes. He wasn't listening." Or slowing down.

"At the first turn, the car started hopping and sliding, and I saw a white picket fence shatter," said Bruce. "The car was on its side. I pulled myself out through the broken windshield and collapsed on the ground. All around me was smoke and confusion." And tilted above him, the nearly two-and-a-half-ton family wagon.

His first instinct: hide the drugs.

"I buried them in the dirt of the garden where we'd crashed," said Bruce. "Cars were stopping, and people were trying to help. It looked like the station wagon was going to fall on me."

Bruce and Scott were taken to GBMC—the Greater Baltimore Medical Center—in the same ambulance. Scott said his jaw hurt, but he was otherwise uninjured. Bruce had a broken back and was in so much pain he thought he was going to die.

As he was rushed into the ER, Bruce glanced into a passing mirror, saw what had become of his face after smashing into the windshield, and began crying. "I had compression fractures of two vertebrae, and my face was severely disfigured," he said. "I went through about six years of plastic surgery."

But first they had to save his life.

"They started working on me, and then a doctor stuck a needle in my leg," said Bruce. "Very quickly all the pain left me. Not just the physical pain, but all of the emotional and mental anguish I'd lived with all my life disappeared. I'd found the answer."

Drifting into a narcotic haze, Bruce had no idea that the stuff in the needle—representing manifold opiates in all their variations—"would become paramount to my existence for the next twenty-nine years."

When Bruce woke up after surgery, his immediate thought was to find out what drug he'd been given that had taken the pain away.

"Instinctively I wanted more."

He told a nurse he was in agony, and a few minutes later she returned with a second syringe. The mere anticipation brought relief. He politely asked the nurse what it was, and she replied, "Morphine."

Bruce began pressing the button that summoned the nurse around the clock. "They'd always tell me it wasn't time for another shot," he recalled. "But I'd tell myself, 'Oh yes, it is.'"

> "My back still hurts. I should have never walked again."
>
> —*Bruce White*

Bruce's grandmother Mernie—the one who prayed for him for years and, in the world to come, begged God to spare him during his near-death experience—cried when she saw the boy all banged up at GBMC. Though he loved Mernie, Bruce wasn't especially moved by her grief.

"I needed another shot," he said.

Bruce stayed at the hospital long enough to learn to walk again before going back to Sheppard Pratt. He arrived in a metal back brace that stretched from below his hips up to his armpits. Hidden in the brace were several syringes stolen from GBMC.

"I didn't know how to use them, but was hoping Chris might," said Bruce. "I had no drugs to put in them, but it seemed like a good thing to have."

Bruce found his roommate—who made some jokes about how banged-up Bruce was—and they went to the group room to hang out.

"It was good to laugh," said Bruce. "And Chris knew how to use the syringes."

But they had nothing to put in them. Months went by, and the syringes remained hidden, unused except for the time Chris tried shooting mouthwash into his arm and wound up with a large abscess.

Psychological therapy continued for Bruce, who persisted in not cooperating, though he learned to play both ping-pong and pool while wearing the brace. Living on a psych ward without being able to get high, he said, "sucked."

Time for Great Escape Part Two, in which Bruce and Chris hatch an ingenious plan: Go to the game room in their heavy jackets, say they both had to go to the bathroom at the same time, and simply run away!

"The staffer escorting us knew it was bullshit," remembered Bruce. "But he didn't do anything about it."

They ran.

Once off campus, Bruce found a pay phone and called a friend of his named Mark Klass (born Joseph Mark Klass; fond of marijuana and LSD, he would take his life in 2012), who showed up in a white-topped, sky-blue Pontiac Tempest—a '63, perhaps a '64.

"We were free," said Bruce, free to get high and drink beer and spend the night in the woods behind a supermarket where a few years earlier he had hunted small birds. "We lay there talking," he said, "looking up at the stars." Just a couple of teenage stoner cowboys adrift in the American 'burbs.

"The only thing missing was our girlfriends, our rehab romances," said Bruce. So, they made another plan to go back to

Sheppard Pratt as soon as possible and spirit away a couple of girls named Arrow and Christina.

They went back to the pay phone the next morning to call Klass and make another run. At 11 a.m., Arrow and Christina were poised to look out for the right moment. Full of breakfast beer and reefer, Mark, Bruce, and Chris pulled up outside a Sheppard Pratt parking lot. Bruce and Chris crouched down while Mark idled between a pair of parked cars.

"A few minutes later we saw the girls running across the parking lot," said Bruce. "They were laughing so hard it was hard to talk to them. It was all a big game."

Klass stomped on the gas pedal of the Tempest, and they headed toward Lutherville and the house of the guy who had been at the wheel when Bruce nearly died: Scott Pettingill.

"Scott's family was away," said Bruce, who was still wearing the back brace when they pulled into the driveway and walked into the house. "I hadn't seen him since the day he left the hospital after the accident."

Bruce and his entourage were welcomed in. The girls began to raid the refrigerator for food, and the boys started getting high.

Though another neighborhood friend—tattoo artist Rene Eibl—said "no one was friends with Scott" after the station wagon accident, Bruce viewed a house free of grown-ups as an opportunity, overlooking that the kid who lived there had nearly killed him.

For the next two days, said Bruce, "all we did was smoke pot, drink beer," and have as much sex as four young escapees could cram into forty-eight hours before Scott told them to leave.

"I was good with that," said Bruce. "I'd had my fill."

Chris and the girls returned to Montgomery County, and Bruce pondered his next move, deciding, "I guess I'll go home."

First, he went to Greg's house, where he swallowed a few Seconal, smoked reefer, and shot pool. The Sheppard Pratt policy was to give away a client's bed if the client was absent for three days. Bruce had been gone for five, "relieved that I wouldn't be going back."

The next morning, he left Greg's house and hitchhiked home to Seminary Avenue, a mile and a half away. The closer he got, the more his stomach churned. His ride dropped him off, and Bruce leaned against a stone wall across the street from his house, smoking a cigarette and getting up his nerve to go in.

"I knew they'd be mad," he said. "But I really didn't give a shit."

The first person he encountered inside was his brother Andy, who stared at Bruce and said, "Mom and Dad are really pissed off."

Still groggy from the barbiturates he'd taken the night before, Bruce sat down and lit another cigarette. His father walked by and, according to Bruce, "looked at me with disappointment, shock, and rage." His mother couldn't stop crying as they sat down for a family meeting.

"I did a good job of pretending I was listening," said Bruce. Charles said that he'd persuaded Sheppard Pratt to take the teenager back, and Bruce bolted for the door, knocking down his mother as she tried to stop him.

A friend of Woody's was at the house and grabbed Bruce before he got out the door. Bruce apologized to his mother, saying he hadn't intended to hurt her.

"Just to shut everybody up I agreed to go back to Sheppard Pratt," he said, where, an hour later, he was restricted to his unit. Chris and the girls were still on the lam, and Bruce proceeded to act like the insufferable jerk that he was when he couldn't get his way.

"My mouth was filthy and my tongue razor-sharp to staff and clients," said Bruce.

In early May, he was taken to GBMC to have his back brace removed. His first steps without it were tentative. "I could bend a little but not very much. From then until now my back has been a source of great agony." (He would break it twice again in the years to come, and some doctors believed he might never walk again.)

By early June 1975—after Bruce spent about five more months in rehabilitation that was supposed to last two years, Sheppard Pratt deemed him "untreatable," and the teenager got his wish—the door.

"They'd had enough of me," he said.

6

Last Chance High

THE BALTIMORE EXPERIMENTAL
HIGH SCHOOL

"We had so many people come into the school from
[psychiatric institutions] that Sheppard Pratt was like
our sister school."

—*Joe Bien, BEHS graduate*

By the time Bruce got kicked out of the psychiatric hospital (he had more important things to do than figure out what was wrong with him), the fifteen-year-old had nearly died in a car crash, spent insurance money from the wreck on motorcycles—Icarus on two wheels—and was beginning to see friends die via all manner of violence and stupidity.

"My folks thought I was just going through a phase," said Bruce. "When we got home from Sheppard Pratt, the only thing my mom asked me was if I wanted something to eat. That's what she did when things were difficult."

All they knew how to do, he said of his frustrated and flummoxed parents, was to look for ways to comfort him. "They dealt with me the same way they had since the second grade," he said.

The reasons Bruce was booted from Sheppard Pratt—where it seemed that attempts were made to address everything but his entrenched addiction—were never discussed. Now, the Whites had to find a school that would take a kid who had already experienced more trauma by age fifteen than most people do in a lifetime.

Where other kids might be grounded for the rest of their lives, sent to questionable boot camps, slammed into another therapeutic institution, or simply kicked out to fend for themselves, Bruce was given a sandwich.

"Thanks, Ma," and out to the garage he ran to ride his 125cc Yamaha dirt bike, which he'd acquired in exchange for narcotics.

But a part of him—the small voice that would half-heartedly seek treatment in high school, a spiritual pilot light, perhaps, not yet extinguished—tried to embrace the summer of 1975 as a fresh start. To that end, he had his hair chopped off.

"It had been almost to my waist," said Bruce of his bushy mane, which grew outward before falling to his shoulders, like the image of Robert Plant on the back of *Led Zeppelin III*. "I had it cut above my ears and combed it straight back."

Charles and Maxine were thrilled, holding out hope that the impulsive act signaled a change for the better. But it was merely cosmetic. Bruce was now an addict with short hair. The same day he saw a barber he joined friends to drink and smoke pot in an abandoned farm building not far from home.

"The year at Sheppard Pratt didn't heal or cure me of anything," he said. "It was all just ramping up."

As Bruce was no longer welcome in the Baltimore County Public School system, the Whites searched for a good school that would take him. After he deliberately failed an entrance exam at Calvert Hall—a prestigious Catholic prep school near his home—they set their sights on any school.

"Zero choices left," said Bruce. "I convinced my parents to let me take a year off."

FIGURE 6
The former Baltimore Experimental High School, near the corner of Franklin and Cathedral Streets. Photo by Jennifer Bishop.

He spent the summer riding his motorcycle around Loch Raven Reservoir and along the railroad tracks in the old part of Lutherville, always high, always able to find other kids who wanted to get high.

Over the summer of 1975, the kid from Lutherville with the drug problem became the kid with a drug problem and a driver's license. With more money from the Christmas night accident he bought a 1971 Mercury Cougar from his older brother Woody. His father said that if he wanted to drive it, he'd have to get a job.

Bruce picked up work as a dishwasher and distinguished himself as a big-shot dropout chauffeur, driving friends to school in a rockin' convertible.

"While they were in class, I would smoke pot and do whatever drugs I could get," he said. When the afternoon bell rang, Bruce picked them up for the after-school buzz on the way home. "Back then," he said, "for $20 you could fill your tank with gas, get a case of beer and some weed, and drive all night."

One day, while riding his Yamaha along the rails—years before commercial development sprawled across his old stomping grounds—Bruce discovered a custom motorcycle shop on Aylesbury Road. The chain on his dirt bike was slipping, and he went in to see if they could help. There, he met a long-haired, self-taught mechanic, a guy with a beard, dirty T-shirt, and engineer boots who liked to get fucked up almost as much as Bruce did. They called him Captain Eddie. Last name Herbert.

"I thought he was about the coolest guy I'd ever met," said Bruce. "It changed my life forever."

Captain Eddie helped Bruce fix the chain—adios dishwashing! The shop immediately became Bruce's hangout, and he immediately adopted the lifestyle of a biker. He swept the floor, washed and waxed motorcycles, and took out the trash for the privilege of learning about hogs and choppers and just being there.

Captain Eddie called him "kid"—a *compadre*—and the shop owner, Dave Erbe, a talented mechanic who would soon factor in a violently pivotal moment in Bruce's life, was cool with having the kid hang around.

"We would go all over the state to other custom shops to get parts for the choppers they were building," said Bruce, who had his eye on an ice-blue, "chromed out" Harley-Davidson Sportster under construction.

"I would have done just about anything to make this motorcycle mine," said Bruce. The moment the bike was finished, he asked his parents for more of his insurance money, bought the Sportster, and never went back to anything smaller than a Harley.

"With my new black leather jacket and engineer boots, I had an identity," said Bruce. "I was a drug addict biker."

The facade put down roots—deep and gnarled—with Bruce's first intravenous shot of heroin in the back of his Dodge Super Bee, his all-time favorite car—"the coolest car I've ever seen," he said. Bruce bought the vehicle at sixteen. A friend would later wreck it.

The leap into the junkie world occurred during his year off from school with Greg Burke—who'd already been shooting dope—and a neighborhood guy from Francke Avenue they called Fat Donald for obvious reasons.

"Donald did it for me," said Bruce of the first of thousands of narcotic injections, a habit that in time would find him shooting cocaine dozens of times a day. "I got sick, threw up, and was so high I had to ride around in the backseat of my own car while Donald drove."

After Bruce's fucking-around sabbatical, his parents found a school that provided a safety net for kids like him (though there weren't many quite like him) and kids who needed a nontraditional atmosphere to get on with life.

On the first day of the '76–'77 school year, a seventeen-year-old Bruce headed downtown from the northern suburbs on an ice-blue Harley Davidson. Destination: 504 Cathedral Street, a former parish house for the Franklin Street Presbyterian Church, around the corner from the Enoch Pratt Free Library headquarters and the Basilica of the Assumption, in the Mount Vernon neighborhood of downtown Baltimore.

Bruce cruised south on Charles Street, "through the big sweeping turns" past two major institutions in his life up to that point: Greater Baltimore Medical Center and Sheppard Pratt psychiatric hospital.

"I could feel the warm sun on my face, and I had my best biker attire on," said Bruce of that September day. "Riding past Hopkins [university], I slowed down to look at the girls and hoped they were looking back at me."

Bruce's parents had learned that some of the kids from Sheppard Pratt were going to BEHS, total enrollment about sixty students. They weren't thrilled with the place, said Bruce, "but I guess they thought it was better than having me hang around bikers all day."

The school opened in the fall of 1970, about the time that George Harrison released "All Things Must Pass" and the Ford Motor Company introduced the Pinto. It closed fifteen years later as the Francis W. Parker School, operating out of the basement of a Baptist church in Northeast Baltimore.

It was a straw—often the last one—for parents to grasp when at their wits' end. And for their kids—teenagers too innocent, naïve, or dim to know how careful one should be about what to wish for—a dream come true. Short of assaulting someone, little was forbidden.

"The culture was both liberating and dangerous," said John W. Wood, who graduated a year or two after Bruce and went on to teach history at a Baltimore-area prep school. "Some of us consider ourselves lucky to have been a part of the school and lucky to have survived it. If you were taking bets on who was least likely to survive, Bruce would have been at the top of most lists."

Yet, for all its faults, said Wood, the school "saved people like me."

If Rock and Roll High School had the Ramones running the glee club, the Baltimore Experimental High School was Woodstock *and* Altamont, just off the corner of Franklin and Cathedral. White pulled his Harley up onto the sidewalk and removed his helmet for the classic Hollywood star turn: Bruce White is here, and he's a cool motherfucker.

"I was never a shy kid, so I started introducing myself," said Bruce, the affable embodiment of the dark side of flower power. On his jacket, a patch with the letters FTW—"fuck the world"—a philosophy somewhat at odds with a school that named its Ultimate Frisbee team "the Fighting Butterflies."

Bruce began each school day parking his motorcycle in a lot behind the building and getting high between the parked cars with the attendant—an older Black man named Bill—and whoever else was hanging around. "The school let us drink in the backyard," said Bruce. "But if you wanted to smoke pot you had to go to the parking lot."

On the inside: "Not many blackboards and no desks," said Bruce. "In some of the classrooms there was nothing but big cushions on the floor."

As the weeks went by, Bruce got to know most of the students and gravitated toward those who were reckless like him, thought they liked narcotics as much as he did, and girls willing to have sex. A handful would become good friends and coconspirators, and several of those would die young.

"The most popular kids here would have been the least popular kids at any other school in the country," said Bruce, who used the school's proximity to the Flag House projects near Little Italy to buy dope. "We were mostly misfits and incorrigibles with some type of diagnosable mental illness."

One well-to-do family in Houston with a problem child was under the impression that BEHS was a boarding school. When the boy showed up, he had no place to live and was taken in by Frederick Rutledge Sr., a BEHS board member who taught history, home renovation, and basic electrical skills. Rutledge was also the father of several BEHS students. One of them, a girl named Nina a year or two younger than Bruce, shared drugs and a bed with White.

"There were always drugs at school, but it really escalated when Bruce showed up," said Nina—now Nina Amaya—a belly dancer and dance troupe member. "He could be nice one-on-one, but he was always about posturing and drugs."

One night, after shooting (pharmaceutical) drugs with Bruce, said Nina, she called her father from a motel to say she was "in a motel room with Bruce and wasn't going to make it home."

Where other fathers might take matters into their own hands or call the cops, Fred did nothing.

"He wasn't the type to tell us what we couldn't do," said Nina, whose brother and fellow BEHS student Frederick "Rick" Rutledge Jr. died in 2014 at age sixty-three from "depression, beer, and drugs," his sister said.

Like many others who knew Bruce in the 1970s and 1980s, Nina "expected Bruce to be dead a long time ago."

In his time at BEHS—receiving credit for the year he skipped plus two years of doing drugs and causing trouble in return for a diploma from the State of Maryland—Bruce robbed pharmacies, started his first methadone program, and, on one occasion, sought treatment.

"The one time I looked for help I went to a place that a friend of mine got into after he got locked up for an armed robbery," said Bruce. "They sent him to Hawaii, and I thought that was pretty cool." The receptionist on duty at that treatment center when Bruce walked in listened to the teenager for a few moments and then began asking questions, including "What are you doing with that flute?"

Bruce explained that he'd stolen it from a car the night before and was going to sell it at Ted's Music store a few blocks away to buy dope.

"The guy started cussing me out, saying I wasn't ready to get clean," said Bruce. "That was the last time I tried to get clean" for the next thirty years.

At BEHS, the hippie kids made pot pipes out of apples and enjoyed the trippy-dippy grooves of LSD and psilocybin mushrooms. Bruce preferred drugs that were harder, dirtier, and more lethal.

"I would always have PCP and pharmaceuticals," said Bruce. "A lot of the kids stayed clear of me because the way I used was different."

A girl from Sheppard Pratt named Claire had also landed at the Experimental High School. She did not stay clear of Bruce, becoming his girlfriend, sharing needles with him. Early in his first year at BEHS, he and Claire shot morphine sulfate in the second-floor bathroom, one of his favorite spots to use at school.

Asked if this pharmacy-quality compound was more potent than street heroin, Bruce replied, "Is aspirin better for a headache than chewing on leaves?"

The last time he saw Claire, the girl with curly brown hair, one of a few to whom he ever said "I love you," was back in 1994 after he got out of prison for the first time. "She was tricking on North Avenue," he said.

The Greatest Party in the World

> "Candy bowls filled with Quaaludes, bottles of Merck Sharp & Dohme cocaine, orgies, and great music. It was crazy and a lot of fun, but the consequences were a motherfucker."
>
> —*Bruce White, high school kid*

Sometime in late 1975 or early '76—Bruce's junior year at BEHS—a select group of students were invited to attend a private party with a young, attractive teacher named Rebecca Keller.

"Becky was beautiful," said Eileen Vorbach Collins, a roommate of Keller's in downtown Baltimore in the early 1970s. "She was short, cute, and vivacious. She dated a lot of doctors."

A part-time instructor enrolled in the graduate school for social work at the University of Maryland in downtown Baltimore, Keller was the only child of working-class parents who lived near Fort McHenry in South Baltimore. Her father was a mailman. At BEHS, she taught drugs and human behavior. Bruce loved her classes, which were conversational, he said, and focused on his favorite subjects: drugs and music and the post-Woodstock youth culture that promised freedom from traditional social mores.

"Becky had a relaxed teaching style," said Bruce. "She had dark hair and dark eyes and a pretty smile, just a beautiful, gentle way about her. To say I was smitten would be an understatement.

"We would talk about drugs and the social ramifications of the sixties and early seventies drug use, how the Beatles changed the world," said Bruce. "I'd never had the conversations we had in her class. My opinion had some value there, and I never had that before either."

More important, said Bruce, "Becky knew I had a heroin problem, but she didn't treat me differently."

Said fellow BEHS classmate Joe Bien, a 1978 graduate, clean and sober since May 2013: "To me Becky was the epitome of healthy drug use, one of those examples of 'successful addicts' that haunted me, helped me believe it was okay to keep getting high."

Bien's constellation of high-flying art stars included the alcoholic Angeleno poet Charles Bukowski, junkie Beat writer (and poor marksman) William S. Burroughs, and the snakebitten Edgar Allan Poe, buried not far from the high school.

"We all had a crush on Becky, but mostly we had a crush on drugs," said Bien. "Of course I was delusional."

During lunch period, Becky would sit in the school's rear courtyard with Bruce and a few other students and talk about a couple of physicians with whom she was enthralled. One was her new lover, the Californian Paul Geshelin, a gifted physician from Los Angeles who graduated with a bachelor's degree from Johns Hopkins University in 1969 before earning his medical degree there in 1972 and then earning a doctorate in microbiology in 1974. Geshelin had postdoctoral fellowships overseas before returning to Baltimore in 1977, Bruce White's senior year of high school. When Bruce met Geshelin, the doctor was interning at GBMC.

The other guy was a psychiatrist known as "Doctor Russell," Keller's former landlord and Geshelin's racquetball-playing and dope-smoking buddy, a peer with great respect for the short physician with dark hair and a mustache.

"Paul received a PhD for his efforts in proving that strands of DNA were actually strung together like a circle of beads," said Russell, who asked that his last name not be used.

"The way Becky spoke about those guys was mystical," said Bruce. "I knew I had to meet them."

It didn't take long. One day at school, Becky told Bruce that her car was in the shop, and might he give her a ride home?

Off they went on Bruce's Harley to a private road near Robert E. Lee Park in the Mount Washington area of North Baltimore, the well-appointed home of Russell, a young psychiatrist from New Zealand working as an exchange resident at the Phipps Psychiatric Clinic of Johns Hopkins Hospital.

Becky was a lodger there, "a beautiful place down a private road with a Mercedes parked in the driveway," remembered White, who stayed for dinner, smoking reefer with Becky afterward. "The coolest place I'd ever been."

His warm welcome into Russell's home and good graces gave Bruce his first access to what he considered "the true hierarchy of the drug world"—the good shit that doctors filch from hospital pharmacies or self-prescribe for recreation.

But Russell—though he would now and again partake in hard drugs with friends—functioned differently from Bruce and Becky and Geshelin, whom he admonished more than once to cool it before he lost his medical license.

"I couldn't understand why anybody with a prescription pad would not use [narcotics] every day," said Bruce. "Russell could do drugs over the weekend and not use again for weeks."

Now living in Europe—having skipped across the pond to Britain sometime in 1981 after things turned ugly with his druggie friends in Baltimore—Russell recalled the good times / bad times as the permissiveness of the Carter '70s became the Reagan '80s of AIDS and crack cocaine.

"Bruce seemed to like and look up to me and my friend Paul Geshelin, who was an exceptional person," said Russell of the physician-scientist, an addict hobbled by hubris.

Countered Bruce: "My ego would like me to think I was influencing [Russell] and Geshelin as well."

Out of some sixty teenagers in the entire BEHS student body, Bruce was one of a half dozen or so who attended drug and sex parties with the twenty-nine-year-old Keller and her physician friends. She and Bruce were already smoking marijuana together when she entrusted him to select a handful of other kids—those deemed cool enough to handle the action—to party with her physician friends.

L.K., then fifteen and in Keller's drug class with Bruce, was one of them. Nearly forty-five years later, she isn't positive if she attended one or several of the parties but believes it was more than once.

The invite led to a morning visit to a big house in the wealthy neighborhood of Mount Washington in North Baltimore. The outing was billed as an off-site class.

"I remembered thinking, 'Why are we here?'" said L., who at the time was living with and caring for her dying mother a few miles uptown from the school. She soon found out.

"We were given tiny little V-shaped vials of stuff to pour into orange juice," she said. It was MDA: 3,4-Methylenedioxyamphetamine, known as the party drug "Molly."

"Becky said it was a hallucinogenic in which your body feels just like your mind," said Bruce. "She said it was one of the most euphoric experiences she'd ever had."

And who among us—whether the tender age of seventeen or eligible for a senior coffee—would not be keen for a taste of euphoria? And then another. Not young L., who, after the drug took effect, found herself alone in the kitchen.

"I could hear that all the showers were on," she said. "Everyone was in the showers together having sex."

Invited to join, she said he didn't really want to "but felt like I was supposed to and wound up having sex with everybody. I remember thinking that I should be enjoying it, but I wasn't. It was an incredibly empty feeling. I can still remember the shame."

Where some point out that Keller would likely have faced jail time if those parties had taken place decades later, L. is more forgiving.

"Who knows why she made the choices she did?" she said in December 2020. "No one really knows where someone else comes from, what their filters are. I'm not saying there shouldn't have been consequences for her actions, but when we forgive we free ourselves."

Bruce, on the other hand, loved the MDA orgies. In this recounting he may be remembering a different student/teacher party from the one L. remembered. Instead of a weekday morning, he remembers a Friday night, also at the house of "Dr. Russell."

"Russell pulled out a pitcher of orange juice," said Bruce of his most memorable evening—on the positive side of the ledger—in the company of the good doctors. "And Paul began dosing our glasses. He said that something in the orange juice would make the high come on better."

Geshelin was an artisan chemist, and his boutique confection was MDA, which by the time it gets to the customer is rarely pure. But Geshelin's batches of the psycho-stimulant were as unalloyed as they get.

"Paul told us what we could expect, and everybody said, 'Cheers!'" remembered Bruce. "We clinked glasses and drank it down."

And rolled onto the launch pad.

"We went outside to walk around Lake Roland, and I was fucking *gone*," said Bruce. "The visual hallucinations were milder than LSD," but the body high was fantastic. "Near the woods we saw K. hanging naked by his legs upside down in a tree and cackling hysterically, his long blond hair hanging two feet down from his head."

The strollers acknowledged the boy with laughter and hellos—"It was just what we needed to set the scene," said Bruce—who kept walking.

"MDA was a very touchy-feely drug, and we all started to get touchy-feely," remembered Bruce. "Everyone was touching and stroking and hugging each other. It was all love and acceptance hippie shit. My whole body tingled with love and acceptance. I'd never had a drug do this to me before."

Time to go inside.

"Everyone knew what we wanted to do, but nobody said it," said Bruce, remembering the walk down the gravel drive to Russell's house. "Once we got in the door, people just started stripping their clothes off."

The master bedroom was furnished with—what else?—a king-size waterbed. Bruce spotted Becky—the partner he most desired while sober and craved most lustfully under the influence—on the carpet. Happily pretzled together with her was the naked, long-haired boy from the tree. Bruce sidled up and joined in.

Thus engaged with the teacher of his dreams, Bruce peeked over to the bed to see Doctor Russell with a boy from his class and wondered—given memories of his childhood molestation amelio-rated by the ecstatic effect of MDA—if he'd have been a willing participant.

"That night I was up for anything," said Bruce. "I don't think I would have said no."

The evening did not end until early in the morning, when people began crashing all over the house.

"When I got up, I needed some narcotics to get me through" the post-MDA jitters, said Bruce. "Russell kindly gave me some." Soon after, Geshelin returned with packages of new syringes and a salutation: "I've got some Demerol if anybody wants to do some."

So, said Bruce, the core of the group—Russell and Becky and Paul and young Bruce—"sat around and shot Demerol until the wee hours. That's when Paul and I bonded because we were the last ones standing."

The first connection between Russell and the high school kid—dubbed "Young Bruce"—was a love of motorcycles. The second, on the same par if not higher, at least for Bruce, was laboratory-grade narcotics.

And beyond that, all of it mixed together: sex, drugs, rock and roll, no rules, and fast machines.

"Bruce introduced me to some of his motorcycle friends. There was a club called 'Dirt That Moves,'" said Russell. "A gang of low-life villains!"

Villains no doubt—a gaggle of gearheads to which the well-educated and comparatively sophisticated Russell, trained to peer into the psyches of the disturbed and the deviant—was much attracted.

The shrink sought Bruce's advice before buying a black Harley-Davidson Sportster to cruise with White (who rode a '55 Harley chopper) and his biker acquaintances. A few weeks later, Geshelin bought a small Yamaha, and the high school kid and the medicine men often rode together.

As for Dirt That Moves, "I rode with those guys," said Bruce of the club built around employees at Custom Cycles, "but I never wore their patches. If I can't be the head of something, I'm not joining."

The self-styled dirtbags frequently butted heads with equally ba-dass bikers, as their onetime leader, Ricky Davis, could attest if he'd not been killed in a head-on collision with a Volkswagen van.

At the time of Davis's death (Bruce believes it was in Florida), Davis had a tattoo of a motorcycle sidecar with the words "Sidecar Sam R.I.P." Sam was Ricky's dog, and in a dust-up with rival bikers at a bicentennial bluegrass festival near Galax, Virginia, called "Stompin' 76," Sam was taken by the opposition, barbecued, and, as Bruce heard it, eaten.

Just one of a thousand fascinating but perhaps too fantastic stories in the bottomless bag of tales Bruce has lived to tell.

When Bruce rolls out another whopper—typically to entertain someone meeting him for the first time—Baltimore defense lawyer Kevin M. Carr rolls his eyes or excuses himself to refill his coffee.

Carr met Bruce when Carr had a law office in a building owned by a fellow Towson attorney sometime in 2009. He was not immediately charmed.

"I could tell right away that Bruce was a criminal and a bullshitter," said Carr, a former assistant state's attorney who knew the look and the talk, having sent more than a few guys like Bruce White to prison before leaving the prosecutor's office for private practice in 2007. "He was very pleased with himself that he drove a Lexus ES-300. I had the newer ES-350," said Carr. "When I told him that his car was nice but they didn't make it anymore, I could tell he was crushed."

And yet . . .

There was something about this dude, said Carr, something fundamentally different from the typical ex-con. Working for one's self, he noted, "is a solitary existence," and the affable White was always around with a sincere "Howya doin'?" and a good word.

"Bruce and I started going out for coffee," said Carr. "Once you peel away the initial layer of bravado and get past the tattoos and the jewelry, I realized I was in contact with a guy of intense spiritual focus."

As a traditional Catholic educated in Catholic schools, Carr initially dismissed Bruce's frequent "God talk" and eyewitness accounts of miracles as a combo of New Age hogwash and jailhouse hocus-pocus.

(One of those miracles, White believes, is his recovery from hepatitis C, a grueling, multiyear process of trial and error until it was eradicated in 2014. The "cure" [his liver continues to be hobbled by cirrhosis] was the result of new medications, but to Bruce—who has used many thousands of syringes over the years, from his toes to his neck—it is nothing short of divine.)

In time, Carr found Bruce's spirituality to be genuine—including White's endorsement of the "be here now" work of Eckhart Tolle—and credits their decidedly non-evangelical conversations with nudging him back to the faith of his childhood.

"He doesn't talk about the war stories with me anymore, they all sort of run together anyway," said Carr. "But he'll never run out of them."

The story of Paul Geshelin and Becky Keller would eventually make the front page of the *Baltimore Sun* (and not because they won awards for healing or teaching) in a series by veteran reporter Karen E. Warmkessel. By then, the summer of 1981, Russell the shrink was long gone from the US.

Told through the professional life of Geshelin, the articles focused on a medical system whose inability to police itself allowed a rogue doctor to pretty much do as he pleased until his behavior led to his lover's death. The prominent, A-1 Sunday headline read: "Self-Regulation Failed . . ."

"The medical society [MedChi, the Maryland State Medical Society]," wrote Warmkessel on June 21, 1981, ". . . knew that Dr. Geshelin was a drug addict." And then she listed the authorities who were also aware of his brazen behavior more than a year before Keller OD'd in his bed on December 27, 1979: the Maryland Commission on Medical Discipline, the state Health Department, the State Police, and the federal Drug Enforcement Agency.

"Becky was highly allergic, allergic to everything," said Vorbach Collins. "She bought expensive cosmetics because they were hypoallergenic."

Sure enough of himself to participate in the Warmkessel stories—posing beneath a tree for a triptych of photographs by April Saul—Geshelin told the paper, "The day that medical license arrived,

I pulled it out of the mailbox and I held it up and just smiled. I said, 'They don't know what they've given me.'

"I knew I was going to abuse it from the moment it arrived."

If Becky was the "better living through chemistry" den mother of wayward students at the Baltimore Experimental High School, the thirty-four-year-old Geshelin—equal parts stunning intelligence and shocking arrogance—was the Pied Piper with pestle and mortar.

Euphoria is rarely—if ever—the last house on the block for an addict. To embrace pure oblivion, nothing beats opiates.

Said Russell, "When Paul wasn't being generous with MDA, he enjoyed dining on a mixture of Quaaludes and wine. Later, he was injecting increasing amounts of cocaine and opiates, which led to his downfall and the death of sweet Becky Keller."

Bruce got the news while dealing barbiturates he'd acquired in a drugstore robbery, selling the pills in the Baltimore suburb of Reisterstown, about twenty miles from downtown. He was at a friend's apartment, impaired on the product he was selling when his girlfriend Claire—who said she'd had the best times of her life at the parties hosted by Russell and Geshelin—called in hysterics.

"She was crying and yelling, crying and yelling: 'Becky was dead!'"

Bruce jumped into his 1970 Ford LTD station wagon—one of scores of vehicles he owned over the years, this one acquired for $100—and rushed to Claire's house: another exercise in speed behind an all-American chariot, the same kind in which he was a passenger just a few years earlier when he broke the windshield with his face.

"I was extremely high, but the information I had gotten had sobered me some. I was going through red lights, speed limits, over 100 miles an hour in this old station wagon," he said, aware the car was going sideways as he exited Interstate 83 at Timonium Road not far from his home.

"I had it floored, and my light was green coming off the ramp when a car pulled out in front of me. I hit it with such force it flipped that old station wagon up in the air and onto its side. It slid to a stop on the other side of York Road."

Again—face torn up. Again, covered in blood. Again, a trip to Greater Baltimore Medical Center to get patched up one more time. After being discharged from the hospital, Bruce used his mother's car to pick Geshelin up.

As they drove to a junkie friend of Bruce's to get high, Paul told White that "the chalk" in the Demerol—a drug designed to be taken orally—very likely went to Keller's heart, noting that she "just fell over dead" from the chair she was sitting in.

The friend—Ricky R.—was about to shoot up when Bruce knocked. "After he heard what had happened to Paul he just handed him the syringe," said Bruce. Leaving Geshelin to his high, Bruce and his friend went downtown to buy more dope.

Claiming he had nowhere to go (having lost his apartment on Rogene Drive where Becky had died after his arrest), Geshelin was invited by Bruce to come and live with him—a man some thought might one day compete for a Nobel Prize moving in with a junkie friend not long out of high school and his parents.

While on Seminary Avenue, remembered Bruce, Geshelin shared his bedroom and was rude and ungrateful to the point where even the easygoing Charles and Maxine were put off. He was also making a scrapbook of the newspaper stories being written about him in the wake of Becky's death. Once one read past all the "brilliant doctor" stuff they were uniformly unflattering.

As Baltimore prosecutors built their case against Geshelin for the death of Keller—police had found the doctor passed out with a needle in his arm when they arrived after a medic wagon carted Becky away—Bruce received a grand jury summons.

Assistant State's Attorney Peter M. Semel—who died in 2017—tried to squeeze Bruce for information on Russell and Geshelin and the sex-and-drug parties attended by minors. Investigators had the name of Bruce's BEHS classmate with whom Russell had sex at the MDA bacchanal, the only kid whose parents had shown up to demand the return of their child.

"It all seemed more like innuendo than fact to me," said Bruce. "When I left I went straight to Russell and told him to be careful."

(Bruce and Russell remain friendly to this day. Bruce visited the doctor in Tuscany in June 2019, where they relived the events of some forty years ago. Returning to Baltimore at the end of the month, Bruce celebrated sixteen years of being clean and sober at a Sunday night meeting of Narcotics Anonymous.)

Paul Geshelin was charged with more than eighty drug-related offenses, including manslaughter, all of which were dropped when he pleaded guilty to possession of narcotics with intent to distribute. At the time, Semel called the deal a good one in that the felony triggered the revocation of Geshelin's medical license.

Geshelin received a five-year sentence and, because of the deference he'd always received as an impressive professional, served less than five months before being released into treatment.

Recounting the case just before his own death, Semel said Geshelin's Achilles' heel was believing he was *always* the smartest person in the room, even when the room was filled with experts on subjects about which Geshelin knew little.

"When we brought him in to be deposed he started off telling us how it was going to go," said Semel at a café near his Baltimore home. The doctor had brought along a nineteen-page statement he'd written to "help" prosecutors to "straighten some of this out."

Which struck Semel as profoundly delusional. At one of Geshe-lin's many court appearances on drug charges in California and Maryland related to Keller's death, a 1981 newspaper account reported Baltimore judge James W. Murphy (1926–1990) as saying, "I'm convinced that if you don't straighten yourself out . . . you are going to end up in the morgue."

"I was one of Becky's pallbearers, with bloody bandages on my head and high," said Bruce, who helped carry his teacher's coffin, with tears on his face. "I remember her mother coming up to me and thanking me. And that was the end of that scene."

Just about. The circus came to a full stop about two years after Becky's death when Geshelin took his life while awaiting a return to prison. Acquaintances in California, where he died, believe he injected cyanide.

Bruce inherited Geshelin's bright-orange 1965 Dodge van with mag wheels that someone with a grudge vandalized.

And Joe Bien—who once mentioned the long-ago drug orgies to L. and was told never to bring it up again—was left with a lesson it would take him years to apply successfully to his own life.

"When I heard that Paul had killed himself," said Bien, "it was the last word on how wrong my ideas about drugs were."

At BEHS, said Bruce, a school field trip put the emphasis on "trip."

"They were unlike any field trip you can imagine," said Bruce, remembering one to West Virginia. "Some church would lend us a big blue bus, we'd all climb on the bus to go wherever they were taking you, and you get plastered."

The outing Bruce remembers most fondly involved a mountain and a tunnel and soaking little postage stamps of LSD in water before shooting the cocktail into his vein. He did so with a sidekick named Whitney—a waifish boy who followed Bruce into a life of guns, needles, and drugstore robberies—and another guy, K.

"Very quickly," said Bruce, "I was peaking on LSD, and we were toast," an especially dark slice buttered with marijuana and PCP. "Everybody on that mountain was drinking [alcohol] or on some type of drug, including the teachers."

The mountain overlooked a train tunnel that passed through a second mountain, and it seemed like a good idea to the kids—all eight miles high, tripping their brains out—to walk along the tracks through the tunnel.

"It was long and curved," said Bruce. "You could see light coming from the other end but not the other side."

Soon they were seeing the light of something else: an oncoming train.

"Everybody had their backs against the wall of the tunnel," said Bruce. "I was so stoned on acid that when the train passed it went into slow motion less than an inch from my nose and seemed to take forever. I was pinned to the wall with fear."

Tripping on LSD with a freight train bearing down on him petrified Bruce. But looking into the barrel of a gun held by someone wishing him ill was just another moment of "here we go."

Of the many memories of the unorthodox approach to education students from BEHS recall, one of the most vivid is the Thursday morning "all-school" assembly designed to air grievances and trade ideas in an open setting. By attending, students earned a "Democratic Institution" credit.

At one of these meetings, school director Kelley Kidd said that syringes had been found in a bathroom trash can on the second floor. Bruce remembers Kidd dumping the can out in front of the students, and along with paper towels came a couple of syringes.

A lecture about the danger of the needles—not the dope, but how someone could be hurt while emptying the trash—"went on and on," said Bruce, "so I stood up and said, 'I did it. They're mine.'"

Satisfied, Kidd reportedly went on to other school business.

At another all-school meeting, said Nina, Bruce took umbrage when her father called him a junkie. Bruce got mad and said, "A junkie can't pay for his habit. I can afford mine!"

Bruce graduated from the Baltimore Experimental High School in June 1978 along with a half dozen or so other students.

"They gave us some kind of fucking diploma," he said of the hand-printed document made by Nina's brother Rick. "It was probably the only kind of school I could have made it through."

From Joe Bien—who believed that Bruce was a good guy unable to escape his worst impulses—White received something that meant more to him than the diploma: a poem illustrated with a caricature of the motorcycle-riding heroin addict called "Bird."

"Ain't got no rhythm / Ain't got no blues / Just keep on livin' / Anyway he choose . . ."

"I had it framed, but somewhere along the line I lost it with everything else," said Bruce, who nurtures fond memories of the odd school for oddballs. "I know I did a lot of damage to a lot of people there, but none of it was done with malice.

"After I left high school, I basically did nothing constructive for the next twenty-five years."

Whitney Denham: His Real Name Was Stuart

> "Whitney was very extreme, that's why we got along
> so well. If he was still here today I would tell him how
> sorry I was that I couldn't be a better big brother."
>
> —*Bruce on his high school best friend*

Stuart "Whitney" Denham—a high school classmate, a quiet boy—kept bugging the biker dude to turn him on to the real shit: dope, junk, heroin. The kid was infatuated with Bruce and the dark world White traveled in.

"I told him he didn't want any part of that life and I wasn't going to be the one to bring him into it," said Bruce, who made no secret of shooting heroin with friends in the second-floor bathroom.

One Saturday morning, Whitney called Bruce and told him to come over, that he had something to show him. Bruce begged off until Whitney told him that he'd just robbed a pharmacy and needed a lesson in what to do with the booty.

"I told him I'd be right over," said Bruce, who hopped in his Super Bee for the ride to the "Hilltop Hotel," the home of a friend of Whitney's in the Forest Park neighborhood of Northwest Baltimore.

On the way, Bruce kept thinking, "This kid has the biggest balls of anybody I have ever met." Yet aside from his ferocious appetite for narcotics—and whatever doubts and demons vexed Denham—the kid Bruce sometimes called "Weebee" was White's opposite in almost every way.

Whitney greeted Bruce at the door with a smile and led him to the haul: lots of barbiturates, a variety of amphetamines, a large bottle of morphine sulfate, a fifteen-grain bottle of Dilaudid compounding powder, and a couple of eighth-ounce bottles of the same.

"It was one of the largest pharmacy scores I'd ever seen," said Bruce, who by that time—age seventeen—had taken part in about two dozen such heists.

Amazed and somewhat baffled, Bruce gave Whitney a funny look and asked, "How did this happen?"

Denham explained that he had tired of asking Bruce to get him high, so he took matters into his own hands "and did what you do," pointing to the eighteen-inch sawed-off shotgun he had used to hold up a pharmacy near Edmondson Avenue while his friend, a kid named Scott, waited at the wheel of a getaway car.

Stuart Denham had gone to Park School, a prestigious K-through-12 prep school in Baltimore, before leaving for the experiment on Cathedral Street. It was sometime during middle school at Park that someone started calling him Whitney because he happened to look like some other kid with the name.

Bruce described Whitney as "about five-foot-seven, blue eyes, and long blond hair to his shoulders. He was only about fifteen years old and not what you would call an intimidating figure." Glancing at the shotgun and then back to the narcotics, Bruce told the rookie stickup man, "I think you scared the living fuck out of somebody."

And then, finally, it was time to reward Whitney and Scott with the fruits of their labor.

"I injected both of them for their first time and saw euphoria cross their faces," said Bruce. "Then I injected myself and sat back to enjoy the high."

From that point on—having earned his merit badge—Whitney was Bruce's best friend and partner in crime and adventure. When they were out of dope and didn't feel like finding the money to buy more, they'd go out and rob a pharmacy the way someone else would run to the 7-Eleven for a gallon of milk.

After one holdup, Bruce was driving the getaway car and didn't see any cops headed to the scene of the crime. Among the drugs they'd just stolen was a bottle of liquid Demerol. Whitney "pulled up a shot" from the bottle with a syringe and handed the needle to Bruce, who injected the drug in his leg with his right hand while driving with the left.

"I always thought," said Bruce, looking back, "that if I ever got arrested leaving a job, at least I would be high."

At one potentially fatal yet rather typical moment, the puppy saved the Big Dog's life.

After one pharmacy robbery, they set up shop—guns and drugs and money—in a long-gone hot-sheet motel called the Pine Ridge

Inn not far from the Ruhl Armory in Towson. Before putting the word out about what they were selling, Bruce and Whitney got high. After several hours shooting opioids and cocaine "speed-balls," along with shots of straight cocaine, Bruce began working the phone.

One interested party was an addict named Jan, a pretty girl who sometimes got high with Bruce and took rides on his motorcycle. She said she was bringing along a guy that Bruce didn't know. The idea of bringing along a stranger didn't sit well with Bruce, but he knew Jan well enough to be okay with it.

(Regarding the quaint notion of honor among thieves, Bruce said, "We all did a little snitching back in the day. I did a little bit—we all did. The further you got into addiction, the more the moral fabric deteriorated.")

Jan said she would hang out with Bruce after the sale, leading him to believe he'd be getting laid that evening, a prospect that led him to let his guard down. She arrived with a man named Tommy—a sleazy-looking man who was physically bigger than Bruce—about 9:30 p.m.

Bruce did business from the desk in the room with a sampling of the drugs. Whitney was in the back bedroom with the rest of the stash. "As far as I knew, he was nodded out," said Bruce.

Tommy began to nitpick the drugs, saying they were fake and he wasn't going to buy. Bruce replied that he didn't give a fuck what the guy thought, "just put my shit back on the table and leave."

"And then I had a gun in my face," said Bruce, who, though un-armed, continued to tell Tommy to go fuck himself.

"I'm looking down the barrel of a small-caliber handgun, and I don't know if it was because I was high or I just had no self-worth, but I don't remember having much fear," said Bruce. "And then I heard words from heaven."

The voice was Whitney's, the teenager Bruce remembers as "a kind and gentle loner, born broken, just like me," a junkie who OD'd more than anyone with whom White shot dope, a kid he'd resuscitated with CPR and ambo calls many times.

In the soft monotone came a threat: "If you don't get that gun out of my man's face I will cut you in half."

Whitney backed up the threat by putting the shotgun up against the man's midsection. Bruce grabbed the gun from Tommy and told him and Jan to get the fuck out.

"At this point," said Bruce, "Whitney and I became one of the most ruthless teams I had the pleasure to be a part of."

Such a long way from the more "flower power" adventures Whitney had with Joe Bien, like the time they hitchhiked to Florida together in search of psilocybin mushrooms.

Whitney was also a solo act and robbed more pharmacies by himself or with someone else than he did with Bruce. For one of these, while still in high school, he was arrested in Baltimore County and held in the Towson jail. While his friend was locked up, Bruce mailed him letters with PCP powder behind the postage stamps.

"It's amazing what you could get away with back then," said Bruce, who would press down on the envelope with his boot to flatten the stamp. "I'd send the letters from different return addresses, they'd deliver it to Whitney in jail, and he'd peel it off and eat it to get high."

When Whitney stood trial, he was sentenced to a drug rehab in Arizona. He wound up relocating to the Grand Canyon State with an addict named L., whose pleasures and kindnesses he shared with Bruce until White tired of her.

Whitney returned to Baltimore a few times—once to be the best man at Bruce's wedding in 1984, after which White only saw his friend one more time. A few years after that, L. called from Arizona to say that Whitney had overdosed again and did not survive.

"Whitney was a good boy," said Bruce. "But it was always about the dope."

In the way that siblings can be raised by the same parents under the same roof and yet turn out as different as apples from avocados, Whitney's brother Schuyler became a Baltimore City police officer.

Schuyler married a Baltimore Experimental High School graduate, retired from the force, and has made a good life for himself and his wife in Colorado, involved there—as he was in Baltimore—in the arts scene.

"I don't know if I can forgive Bruce," said Schuyler, noting that his father deemed White "not worthy of his attention" and did not want to talk. "But I am curious—have you found anyone with anything nice to say about him?"

7

Spanish Harlem

THERE COULD HAVE BEEN BLOOD

"Blood was its avatar and its seal—the redness and the horror of blood."

—*Poe, "The Masque of the Red Death"*

O ne day in late January of '78—about a year after Bruce graduated from high school—he and Fat Donald headed to New York City in a midnight-blue Corvette owned by another junkie. They were loaded with $3,500 in cash and a .38 snub-nosed revolver for an adventure in Harlem, said Bruce, that neither would ever forget. Their destination was the tenement apartment of a guy known as Panama.

Bruce had been going to New York regularly in his late teens and early twenties to get dope, sometimes twice a week. Occasionally, he bought records and clothes that weren't easy to find in Baltimore. Once in a while he brought backup muscle, like Fat Donald, the guy who first put a needle in his arm. Always, he returned with narcotics.

"On the way up, Fat Donald and I were smoking joints and joking a lot," said Bruce. "We had both shot some smack before we left Baltimore. We had a big bag of marijuana. We were driving a borrowed Corvette. Things were cool."

FIGURE 7

Bruce and Cynthia Levering, the mother of his daughter. They are passed out on heroin, the state White craved. His mother took this photo in an attempt to shame him into getting straight. Source: Bruce White.

Cool is what Bruce expected in his dealings with Panama—"quick as usual—in and out and back on the road before it got dark."

Panama did business from his family's fifth-story walk-up on 119th Street. A winding staircase inside an old brownstone, late nineteenth-century architecture, and a bit of wariness on Bruce's part as he approached the apartment's door. Bruce had called Panama several times from pay phones on the turnpike, but the dealer had not answered.

Once there, said Bruce, "I heard the familiar sounds of the deadbolt and door brace letting go. Panama greeted us warmly. I introduced Donald, and we went in and sat down."

Off a dark hallway was a room where Panama "did business and people would shoot up," said Bruce. On the other side, maybe ten feet away, was the kitchen, its doorway hung with long strands of plastic beads. From the kitchen came sounds of Panama's family—perhaps a friend or two, about four or five people—speaking Spanish and laughing

Bruce told Panama he was looking for an ounce of cocaine and several "bundles" of heroin, about twenty-five nickel bags of junk in each bundle that he could sell for fifteen dollars apiece back in Baltimore.

Panama took some money from Bruce and ran out to get the "testers" that would let White know if the shit was worth the price. Panama returned with a variety of heroin and coke from which Bruce mixed up small shots, sharing with Donald.

The Baltimore boys were in agreement on what they liked best, and Bruce gave Panama the rest of the $3,500. The New York dealer said he'd be back in about forty minutes.

"We were happy to wait," said Bruce. "If Panama took his time, we had plenty of drugs to do until he got back."

But Panama did not come back as promised. An hour passed and then two, and Bruce said to Donald—late in the afternoon, two white boys in black Harlem, "He's never been this long before."

They shot some more dope and continued to wait. "I'm high, I nod out, and when I wake up it's dark and snowing outside," said Bruce. Several more hours had passed.

"I said, 'Fuck this, this cocksucker ain't stealing my money. I told Donald to give me the gun and sat there with the .38 in my hand. I knew this motherfucker had ripped me off."

Donald asked Bruce what he was going to do. "If he's not here soon," said Bruce, staring through the beads that separated the sitting room from the kitchen, "I'm going to murder his whole family."

Donald, near tears at the prospect, considered this in silence before telling Bruce that he could not be part of it, that if
Panama didn't come back soon they should just catch up with
him later. To which, according to Bruce, he replied, "I will leave
a bloody mess!"

More time passed, no Panama, and Bruce told Donald that they
were leaving. Bruce walked into the hallway that led to the kitchen
and peered through the beads from about eight feet away.

"I had the piece at my side, cocked, trying to decide which
[person] to start with," said Bruce. "I saw two heads, one with its
back to me talking to someone across from them. I thought about
shooting the one closest to me and then doing the other one."

As Bruce pondered committing multiple murder, he heard the
front door unlock, released the trigger, and put the gun back in his
pants, screaming at Panama, demanding to know why it took so
long. Panama was in the company of two white men, and Bruce
instinctively knew they were cops.

Panama began attempting to give the packages of dope he'd
brought back with him to Bruce, and Bruce kept refusing. "They
aren't mine," he said, heart pounding against his ribs as the white
guys kept trying to get him to take the narcotics.

"There was nothing okay about this," remembered Bruce.
"I walked outside of the apartment into the hallway, and Panama
followed me with the bag. I put the gun under his chin and said,
'I'll blow your fucking head off if you say a word.'"

At that moment, said Bruce, "Panama saw me for who I was."

Bruce grabbed the bag of dope and ran down five flights of stairs
with Donald behind him, only to discover that the snow was so
deep they had to force the doors of the Corvette open.

"I started rocking the Corvette to get it out of the parking
spot, and when I looked up there was a van in front of me with

the door open and several cops getting out," said Bruce. "One had a shotgun on us."

Being fat has its advantages. "Donald was a very large man, and tonight his weight was a blessing," said Bruce—the big man had stashed the bag of narcotics under his belly. Standing at the driver's-side door, the sergeant began screaming in Bruce's face: "This guy ain't nothing but a junkie" and tried to force the sleeves of Bruce's brown leather jacket up to reveal needle tracks.

"The sleeves wouldn't go up because my arms were so swollen from shooting dope," said Bruce. "I was in total fear."

The captain then began debating with the sergeant regarding Donald, saying, "The fat fuck ain't no junkie."

And Bruce began repeating a mantra of bullshit: "We're just out-of-towners at a convention looking for pussy."

With the dope hidden between the folds of Donald's stomach, the cops searched both men and came up with a bag of weed in Donald's pocket. They were also running the registration on the Corvette. "This is Harlem," one of the cops told Bruce. "You're going to get killed."

To which Bruce said they were just driving around looking for pussy and they got lost.

Twenty minutes later, the captain—believing the reasonable lie Bruce had told—put the marijuana back in Donald's pocket and told the hapless conventioneers to get their idiot asses home.

"We began heading south on Broadway, and tears were streaming down my face," said Bruce. "If the sergeant and the captain hadn't been arguing about whether or not we were junkies we'd have gone to prison."

Turning to Donald as they drove into Manhattan, Bruce said, "I thought the gun and the dope were under your stomach."

To which Donald replied, "Only the heroin would fit." The cops had not found the gun.

"All we wanted to do was pull over and get to a place where we could shoot some dope and relax," said Bruce. "I stopped at the Americana Hotel on Fifty-Ninth and Broadway, a fancy joint once upon a time that would cost more than I wanted to spend, but I didn't care."

They entered a lobby filled with couples in gowns and tuxedos, well-heeled guests who stared at the young, very lucky criminals. A room was $125, a lot of money in the late 1970s. A bellhop carried Bruce's small leather bag, but Bruce was not in the mood for courtesies.

"When I told him to just take us to the fucking room, I thought he was going to shit himself," said Bruce. "Once we got in the room, we got high the rest of the night. The next morning, we drove back to Baltimore."

8

Big Fucking Indian

"I was a kind kid, I was a good kid."
—*Bruce White on the pupa that became a predator*

Somewhere along the line—late in his senior year of high school or not long after graduation—Bruce became acquainted with the Grove brothers: Dale and Gary, a couple of suburban rednecks.

"We were in the same line of business," said Bruce. "We both robbed pharmacies."

One day, Gary told Bruce he had a line on bottles of Dilaudid compounding powder. Bruce got together $1,500—"a very good price" for an eighth of an ounce, he said—and made plans to pick up the goods later that evening.

Bruce picked up a high school buddy—K.K.—in the Super Bee, and they went to see Gary Grove at his apartment in Cockeysville. As they neared the complex at the top of a hill, Bruce told K.K. that "Custom Dave," his buddy from the motorcycle shop, lived nearby.

Inside the apartment were Dale and Gary, Gary's wife, and a guy Bruce didn't know who said his name was John. Against his better instincts, Bruce gave "John" $750, K. did the same, and at 7 p.m. the middleman left, promising to be back in an hour with the Dilaudid.

FIGURE 8

An especially brutal fight over drugs and money in the late 1970s was a turning point for Bruce, shown here in 2014, a moment when he realized that violence was almost as much of a high as drugs—and that the combination made for special pleasure. Photo by Jennifer Bishop.

"I never like to front money before getting the product," said Bruce. "But since I was in their house and Gary's wife was there, I figured it would be okay."

An hour passed, and no John. When Gary told Bruce to be patient, White gave K. a look that said "Did I just lose $750?"

After another hour, Bruce and K. were told to come back in the morning for drugs they had already paid for. When Dale couldn't look Bruce in the eye, "I knew I'd been set up," said White.

Getting up, Bruce told K. to stay put, told Gary he was going to smoke a cigarette and take a walk to clear his mind, "to think about what just happened." He made straight for the apartment at the bottom of the hill: the home of "Custom Dave" Erbe, a well-known biker in his early thirties.

At the door, Bruce could hear a party inside, and once welcomed in, he told Dave he had a problem "up the hill" and needed help. After explaining the situation, Erbe called over a guy known as BFI: "Big Fucking Indian."

"And he was big," said Bruce, who didn't know the man except to say hello at parties. "About six-foot-seven and 280 pounds of solid muscle."

BFI had been smoking PCP, drinking rum and Coke, and was up for some fun. He motioned for a friend to join him, and, in the company of men who enjoyed a good fight, Bruce walked back to the Grove apartment.

"Marching up that hill," he said, "I felt like a king with his army."

When Gary opened the door, BFI grabbed a handful of the guy's hair, lifted him off his feet, and threw him down. While BFI had his foot on the side of Gary's head, the other guy (Bruce never knew his name) knelt down and began slicing Gary's ear with a knife, shouting, "We want the fucking money and the drugs now."

Gary's wife was screaming, Dale sat in horror, unable to speak, and K. began screaming for them to stop, that he didn't care about the money.

"I told [K.] to sit down and shut the fuck up," said Bruce. The assault continued for a few more minutes.

BFI hauled Gary up from the floor, threw him in a chair, and told him to get on the phone to "make it right" or more blood would spill. He backed up the threat by demanding to know where Gary and his wife worked, making it clear that he'd show up there as well.

When Bruce asked his new friends what he owed them for their services, they said it was their pleasure—a friend of Dave's was a friend of theirs. (Their friend—David Cummins Erbe, a University of Maryland graduate with a degree in business—would die a dozen years later at age thirty-seven. His obituary said the death was preceded by a "brief illness" for which he was hospitalized. That illness, said Bruce, was liver failure due to abuse of alcohol and PCP.)

"The giant walked down the hill with his buddy like it was nothing," said Bruce. "Like it had just been a walk in the park."

Back in the apartment, Gary was bleeding from his ear onto his back and shoulder as his wife tried to patch him up. Invigorated by the violence and how it had spared him from looking like a chump, Bruce spoke to the Groves like a drill sergeant, demanding to know if there was anything else he needed to do to get his money back.

K. was repulsed, and Bruce was enthralled. The incident pretty much ended their friendship. Early the next morning, both of them were reimbursed.

It was a turning point for Bruce, a moment when he realized that the violence was almost as much of a high as drugs and that the two of them together made for special pleasure.

In middle school he was always up for dangerous hijinks and never backed down from a confrontation. "Bruce would fight you in a minute, and we watched him hurt people," said Rene Eibl, a childhood friend and classmate. "One of the craziest things was when he shot up the back door of a Chinese carryout at the shopping center where we hung out. "When the cops came, Bruce threw an M-80 under the police cruiser. It scared the shit out of the cop, and we ran away."

But the drama with the Grove brothers and the Big Fucking Indian was not mere delinquency. It contrived to make some of Bruce's core issues—anger combined with ego combined with not giving a fuck—vibrate at a higher level.

"It fueled me," he said. "And I began perpetuating it."

9

Bonnie and Clyde

"Patti went along with any idea I came up with to
make money and get high."

—Bruce White

By September of 1980, two years out of high school, Bruce
had been strung out on narcotics for several years, "a day-to-
day maintenance addict," he said. "Dope sick by mid-afternoon if
I didn't get what I needed."

Methadone—which he began taking in high school—took
the edge off. Traces of PCP in his urine kept kicking him out of
methadone programs. At a clinic in East Baltimore—the old City
Hospitals on Eastern Avenue in Highlandtown—Bruce met the
only love of his life that could not be taken intravenously.

"She was in front of me in line—a blond vision in a T-shirt: 'Peppermint Pattie, Get the Sensation.'"

It was an experience—a candy-bar tease on the shirt of a chick
Bruce found captivating—that he was intent on getting.

Patricia Faith McCormick was a young drug addict and barmaid
who, like Bruce, was dependent on methadone while still using
street drugs.

"I waited for her, leaning against my motorcycle and doing my
best James Dean," said Bruce. "When she got out, I asked if she

needed a ride home, and she said she was taking the bus. It took a minute, but I convinced her to ride with me."

Perhaps she should have gotten on the bus. The ride with Bruce—first back to the White home to pick up liquid morphine and then to Patti's apartment to "hang out and get high"—ended with finality for her four years later.

It led to armed robberies of pharmacies and drug dealers, constant abuse of narcotics, prescription forgery, failed pregnancies, rafts of PCP, marriage, long days of dealing with a psychotic boyfriend, and, on the same motorcycle she'd so eagerly hopped on the morning she met Bruce, her death.

"I spent the night the first day we met," said Bruce. "The next morning, we rode back to the [methadone] clinic on my Harley. A couple of days later, I got down on one knee in a Dunkin' Donuts parking lot and asked her to marry me. She said yes."

And continued to say yes to pretty much anything and everything Bruce proposed.

"We were a toxic couple, but we truly cared about each other," said Bruce. "We couldn't stand to be around normal people because it reminded us of what we weren't."

They were deviants in love; partners in crime, dope, and sex, and sometimes all three in the same hour; a couple of lost, dangerous souls infatuated with firearms and each other.

According to Bruce, "Patti was the most kind and gentle spirit I'd ever met—a loving and giving woman, a much better person than me."

It didn't take much to be a better person than Bruce White back in the day. Like the best molls of yore, Patti stood by her man. "She'd drop you without a second thought if she thought you were going to hurt me," said Bruce. "If you got between me and Patti, you'd lose."

FIGURE 9
Bruce and Patty at the wedding of Bruce's brother Andy. Source: Bruce White.

What would you expect from a woman who claimed to be a de-
scendant of the McCoys, famed for their late nineteenth-century
feud?

Bruce and Patti immediately began living together—bouncing
between Patti's apartment in the Southwest Baltimore neighborhood of Irvington and Bruce's parents' house—and were soon robbing pharmacies together.

"Patti drove my white Dodge van I went in," said Bruce of one job he'd pulled, going in wearing his motorcycle helmet, a note in hand listing the narcotics he wanted, and walking out with a bag of drugs.

"We were both nervous but had no money or drugs, and so I had to get this done," said Bruce. "The pharmacy was about to close. I told her I'd be out in a few minutes and keep the motor running."

Putting on his helmet once more, Bruce entered the pharmacy, showed the gun, and read off what he came for. The druggist filled the bag and went to open the cash register.

"I told him I didn't want money," said Bruce. "Just the drugs."

In the van, Bruce put his helmet in the back, his handgun on his lap, and, as Patti squealed away, told his sweetheart to slow down so as not to attract undue attention. They made it home with a cornucopia of pharmaceuticals Patti had never seen before.

"I showed her how to scrape off the DEA numbers," said Bruce. "If the house was raided they couldn't prove where the drugs had come from."

Then they conducted inventory, and Patti became "very excited—almost childlike"—at the variety. The haul had netted, among other prizes, one of a dope fiend's favored sugarplums—about ninety tablets of pharmaceutical cocaine with a line carved into each of them to be broken in half.

"I'd been involved in more than one hundred pharmacy robberies," said Bruce, "and I'd never seen anything like them before or since."

Bruce broke one of the thick round tablets, crushed the halves, and put the powder in the back of the syringe. He pulled water into the syringe and shook it, noting that "one drop on the end of a needle and the whole room was perfumed with cocaine."

Upon injection: "My ears began ringing with the sound of crashing glass."

Convulsions!

Death by euphoria!

"I'd always believed you could do one of anything and be okay, but I was wrong on this one, it almost killed me," said Bruce. And he loved it. "Cocaine had never done this to me before. I guarded the rest of the tablets—they were for me and Patti and no one else."

The flip side of euphoria is despair, and things got ugly quickly for Bruce and Patti. Then they got uglier.

In November of 1980, a little more than a month after they'd met, Bruce was woken up by Patti's roommate who was yelling, "Patti's been arrested with your gun! She tried to shoot a cop!"

Though it was her day off from serving drinks at Peddlers Pub near her Augusta Avenue apartment, Patti decided to hang out at the bar and have a few while Bruce slept, or, more likely, was passed out.

Patti had been arrested at the pub with Bruce's .22 Ruger. Whether she pointed it at the Southwestern District cop, as the charges stated, is not known, for she was in a blackout when arrested. What was not disputed is that Patti had dated the cop who locked her up before she'd met Bruce.

"She looked pretty beat up when I bailed her out of City Jail the next day but didn't remember anything," said Bruce. "As soon as she got out we moved into my parents' house."

Life for the lovebirds did not calm down or become more acceptably middle class on Seminary Avenue, even though Patti enjoyed chatting with Bruce's mother and would help out here and there.

"She cooked and cleaned and became part of our family right away," said Bruce. "Her and my mom would sit and talk for hours."

When Patti wasn't being the perfect daughter-in-law-to-be, "we'd hit a pharmacy here and there," said Bruce, describing the anxiety that preceded a hit as "the kind of nervousness that lets you know you're alive."

Both of them sold drugs—together and separately—and both were addicted to methadone. Every now and then, Patti would muse about kicking dope and getting clean, thoughts that troubled Bruce.

"I knew I couldn't get clean and had no idea what would happen to us if she got clean, so I ignored it," said Bruce. "She'd bring it up again, but then a good drug deal would come our way, and she'd focus on that."

Patti also wanted to have another child and had stopped using birth control. Bruce didn't like the idea, but he didn't mention it. They had already ended one pregnancy, and Patti barely survived the procedure. On July 28, 1984—nearly four years after he proposed outside the doughnut shop—they were married at the White family home.

His high school buddy Whitney Denham served as his best man, and the guests were a mix of addicts, bikers, ex-cons, and judges, businessmen, teachers, and other upstanding citizens who socialized with Charles and Maxine.

A long row of Harley motorcycles were parked around the White home, and a judge in the crowd told Bruce's father he was pretty sure he'd sentenced more than one of the guests to prison.

(And the guy at the wheel of the kamikaze station wagon in the Christmas Day wreck thought it would be a good idea to crash the reception. Bruce threw him out.)

First thing on the morning of the wedding, Whitney and Bruce started smoking PCP, having partied all night and needing a stimulant to make it through the big day. Aunt Gwen came from

Delaware to do the flowers. By the time his bride arrived, Bruce was swooning through a drugged haze.

"I was so in love with her and truly wanted to be with her forever," he said. "We had one of those once-in-a-lifetime loves you hear about in songs."

The ceremony was officiated by Bruce's old high school teacher Fred Rutledge. Their vows were written by Patti.

"Everybody looked so happy, and Patti and I were smashed," said Bruce. "Whitney was so fucked up he could barely talk but had a great boyish smile on his face. He had trouble giving the toast, so I stepped in. We toasted, somebody hit the tape player, and everybody started to dance."

Patti didn't have much money of her own but was able to get enough together to give her husband a Rolex watch. "No matter how bad things got, no matter how broke or desperate," said Bruce, "I never thought of pawning it."

The newlyweds stayed in town that night, deciding to hang out for a couple of days and honeymoon later. Patti was passed out from drinking methadone all day when they pulled up to the hotel, and Bruce feared she would overdose.

Carrying his bride to their room, he put her on the bed and—"extremely worried"—came up with a plan to revive her that would only occur to a hardcore drug addict.

"I rolled a couple joints of PCP and started shotgunning the smoke into her mouth," he said. I knew the PCP would counteract the methadone, and soon I could see her inhaling and exhaling. An hour later she was coming around, and soon she was talking to me."

And that, said Bruce, "is how our married life began."

Over Labor Day weekend of 1984—on Saturday, September 1, a little more than two months after their wedding—Bruce and Patti went on a motorcycle run with Bruce's biker friends. They met in the parking lot of Sheppard Pratt, drank methadone, and decided to ride to Cumberland, about 140 miles away.

"I drank an extra bottle of methadone and downed a couple Valium," said Bruce. "Patti had a couple pills too. We got on our bikes and started following one another."

By the time the convoy reached Interstate 70 headed west—with at least three hours to go—Bruce was feeling woozy. "I was afraid I'd taken too much," he said. "As always, I ignored it."

About an hour later, he said, "I could feel myself nodding, and Patti nodded out on my back. I pulled up beside another biker and said I can't keep going."

The guy told Bruce to get off at the next exit, that I-70 was well traveled by the police, and, as Bruce recalled, "with a lot of guns and drugs on us, it could be a problem."

The next turnoff was Hancock. "I thought I could make it," said Bruce. "I was wrong."

Passing out, he hit a guardrail at about 70 mph and woke up on the highway to the sound of his cycle running, rear wheel spinning. His only head covering was a bandana, and the skin on his arms was burned away from sliding on the asphalt.

"I looked for Patti," he said, "but I couldn't find her."

When Bruce tried to stand up, one of his shinbones came through his right leg near the ankle. He fell back on the ground and lay there, with no idea of what had happened to his wife. As he pulled off his bandana, blood streamed down his face and chest. He tried to get up again, and a female state trooper put her hand on his chest for him to lie flat.

The cops asked Bruce what happened, and he said he'd been cut off by a car and hit the guardrail. "I told everybody I was run off the road, but that was a lie," he said. "I was the only one who knew what really happened."

A medic helicopter took them both to the hospital in nearby Hagerstown. Upon arriving, they were taken to different rooms. As doctors worked on Bruce, he kept asking about Patti. All he was told was that she was still alive. Several days later, still in the hospital, Bruce got an update on his wife.

"She was in a coma and five weeks pregnant," he said. "I was in absolute despair. Visitors came, and I was glad when they left. At night, I talked to one of the male nurses for hours and cried. I never felt so lonely or ashamed."

When Bruce was allowed to see Patti, it was god-awful.

"She had a big gash on her head where it hit the guardrail, and her leg was broken, same as mine," said Bruce, who held his wife's hand and prayed—to God and whatever else "might be out there"—that she would recover.

"Then they'd take me back to my room," he said. "The nurses put wet compresses on my arms and legs so my skin would grow back from the road [burns] all over my body. It was unbearable. I couldn't move my right arm at the elbow for several days, until a doctor came in and pulled a rock out of it."

Ten days after the crash, on September 11, a physician came into Bruce's room accompanied by a priest.

"They told me Patti was brain dead and had miscarried," said Bruce. "They asked me what I wanted to do, and I told them to unplug the machine."

A few hours later, Peppermint Patti was gone at the age of twenty-eight.

"I'd never felt so bad about anything I'd ever done before," said Bruce. "She had more heart than most of the men I ran with."

Patti's funeral was conducted by the man who had married her and Bruce, Fred Rutledge. Bruce attended in a wheelchair. At the time, he was undergoing skin grafts at Union Memorial Hospital at Calvert and Thirty-Third Streets—where Al Capone was treated for syphilis in 1939—and also received operations on his right leg.

(As a result of the crash, Bruce lost more than a half-inch of length in his right leg, a measurement that became two-and-a-quarter inches after violence still to come. Ever since, the soles on his right shoes have needed padding to even up with the left side. His nickname in some circles is "Big Boot.")

At Patti's funeral, he recalled, "My friend Dinky came in and gave me a hug that ripped a graft completely off my shoulder. I let out a scream, and everyone looked at me. Then Dinky and I went outside to smoke PCP."

At the burial, Bruce put Patti's teddy bear in the coffin along with the leather vest he was wearing in the fatal crash.

Patti's death—and Bruce's direct role in it—created "shame and anger [that] would fuel my behavior for years to come," he said. "The guilt felt like acid."

"I've dreamed about her a few times," he said years later. "They weren't good."

From Patti's death forward, he said, "I couldn't be without drugs for five minutes. I became insane, very aggressive, and smoked PCP constantly to feel invincible—animalistic really.

"Death stopped affecting me, and nobody wanted to fuck with me."

The Animal Becomes a Father

A little less than four years after Patti and her fetus died in the accident for which Bruce was responsible, a woman he'd become involved with—a relationship of drugs, cons, thieving, and violence, the same love song White had been singing for years—gave birth to a baby girl.

On April 28, 1988, Nicole Maxine White—her middle name in honor of Bruce's mother—was born to an addict father who cared little for anyone but his extreme appetites, and an addict mother who wasn't much, if any, better.

"My mom loved Nikki and called her 'Sweet Patoots,'" said Bruce. "Having a baby made it easier to get money out of my family."

The baby's mother was Cynthia L. Levering, a woman from East Baltimore whom Bruce did not love and had not planned to impregnate. "Cindy was stunningly beautiful, and she knew how to work doctors to get pills," said Bruce of the attraction.

Bruce and Cindy (who had an older daughter when she met White) tried the best they could—as a couple of unemployed junkies—to make a family for their daughter. It didn't amount to much more, said Bruce, than paying the rent and keeping the lights on.

They separated when Nikki was about eighteen months old— "I came home one day, and Cindy was having sex on the couch with some guy," said Bruce of their estrangement. The child's day-to-day care largely fell to Cindy's mother, Diane Conti Dressel.

"I've never met a darker soul in my life than Diane," said Bruce. Having pretty much only been associated with dark souls from the time he left high school until his parole from prison, Bruce's appraisal of his daughter's grandmother is rather astounding, if not somewhat hyperbolized.

Now long dead, Diane, Bruce said, "wore gaudy jewelry and a blond Dolly Parton wig. I guess I admired her as a good hustler. She sold drugs with her children, sold stolen property, and sat around planning their next crime."

One of those crimes would be her daughter Cindy's last— a November 1990 robbery that resulted in the shooting death of Harold L. Webb, seventy-five, at his home in Sparks, Maryland.

The plan was simple and stupid: Levering, then twenty-eight, and an ex-lover named Thomas Crawford—age thirty, of Gardenville at the time—would knock on the door of the Webb home and say they had run out of gas and needed to use the phone.

The botched robbery that followed resulted in Levering's conviction for shooting Webb five times. Crawford was also convicted of homicide after each blamed the other. When the jury brought back the guilty verdict against Levering—who had abandoned an original alibi of playing pool at a bar the night of the murder and was found to be the one who pulled the trigger—her mother fainted.

Since March 1991, Levering has been serving a life sentence plus seventy-five years for the murder of Harold Webb, the man who believed she was in distress and allowed her to come into his house to get help.

10

Shootout on Ready

"I've been through a lot, but this was the pinnacle of
my gangster shit."

—*Bruce White*

It was late 1989. Bruce—now the father of a one-year-old he
didn't see very much—isn't sure exactly which month, but the
weather was cold, and he was living in the attic of a house his childhood friend Greg Burke had acquired to grow marijuana indoors.

"We had a grow farm to harvest indica buds," the kind that pro-
duce a deep sense of physical relaxation along with the high. "We
were doing three crops a year, maybe seven or eight pounds a crop,
and selling for $3,200 a pound."

But marijuana was not the buzz either of them craved. One
night, the lifelong compañeros were sitting around shooting cocaine, ran out, and decided to venture out to find more. They were
living on Woodbourne Avenue, a rough side of the Govans neighborhood in North Baltimore, an area anchored by Saint Mary of
the Assumption Catholic Church and which has steadily declined
in the years since Bruce and Greg lived there.

Without money to get the only thing a junkie craves—*more!*—
they put Greg's big-ass, old-school TV with fake wood-grain finish

in the back of Bruce's Thunderbird and went around the corner from Ready Avenue to an open-air drug market.

A couple of white boys trying to trade a used TV for dope. Chumps, right?

Bruce's T-bird was aqua blue, a hot ride he bought from a pawn shop guy for $3,200. The Ford bore the license plates of a Mercedes owned by Greg's mother. One of the young corner chiefs came up alongside the driver's side of the car, put a gun in Bruce's face, and told him and Greg to get out.

"The dude got into the driver's seat, and Greg got back in the car, saying he had to get his schoolbooks out of the back. Greg loved math, he was always doing calculus for fun," said Bruce.

"When the guy put the gun to Greg's head, I took the Buck knife I had in a sheaf on my belt and hit him twice in the chest. First time I hit ribs, and the blade stopped. The second time it went past his ribs and crushed bone. He yelped and dropped the gun."

The weapon fell to the street, and Bruce was able to grab it. "I shoved him into the steering wheel and shot him in the back of the head," said Bruce, who also fired a few shots at a couple of guys accompanying the dealer. None returned fire.

"I flopped the guy out of the driver's seat and onto the street," said Bruce, still in possession of the gun that had been used to threaten him, "and me and Greg drove a couple of blocks back home."

While any reasonably sane person—even a hard-headed criminal—would have left the neighborhood, Bruce persuaded Greg's mother to buy him a shotgun—a Model 870 Remington. He also acquired an extra clip of bullets for the .25 caliber handgun he'd taken from the man who attacked him in the failed TV-for-cocaine deal. Years later, Greg told Bruce that he thought he saw the guy on the street and it appeared that the man's "jaw had been blown out."

FIGURE 10
Bruce (*left*) and brother Andy in Ocean City, Maryland, in 1969. Some twenty years later, Bruce would be shooting a drug dealer in the jaw to escape a deal gone bad. Source: Bruce White.

A day or so after Bruce fired the bullet that ripped through the man's jaw, the dealer's posse came back, ambushing Burke's house on Woodbourne.

"We knew they were coming, so we barricaded the front door and boarded up some of the windows," said Bruce of the shootout, which he said lasted about seven or eight minutes. "They were standing on the porch firing in. A bullet missed my head by six inches."

During the shootout, Greg was upstairs with a woman and no help. "By the time he came downstairs, they'd all left," said Bruce.

When the cops arrived—above the house in a helicopter and a SWAT team at the door—they saw a bullet-riddled house and took Bruce's word that it was self-defense.

Sloppy police work? Was the benefit of the doubt given to an obvious lowlife because he was white?

"It was just very obvious that we were not the aggressors, even though I looked like a junkie and talked like a junkie," said Bruce. "And I'm sure the fact that I'm white didn't hurt. They let me go."

A few days later, a different cop pulled up behind the Thunderbird while it was stalled on the side of the road. The T-bird was turbocharged—"Hit that button and motherfucker *took off*," marveled Bruce—but on this day, the motherfucker could not make it from Govans to Bruce's parents' house in the 'burbs. It was a Thursday or a Friday, and while climbing a hill, the car stalled, and Bruce drifted onto the shoulder. As he tried to start the car, a police cruiser stopped behind him.

The cop asked for license and registration—Mercedes plates on a Thunderbird, "that's a hard one to explain," said Bruce—and told him to get out of the car. Like a strung-out gunslinger out of Tombstone, Arizona, White was wearing a tan leather duster with his long, unruly hair greased back in a ponytail.

"I'm a tall, skinny guy, I'm loaded, and I truly don't give a fuck," said Bruce. "I was just going to my parents because I needed to take a break for a little while."

When the officer asked Bruce to open the truck, "the first thing he saw was the shotgun," said Bruce. "He immediately shoved me onto the trunk of the car and started searching me as backup arrived."

The arresting officer took the .25 pistol from Bruce's pocket, and Bruce was shipped off to the Baltimore County Detention Center, where, as he was processed, they found his stash of fake prescriptions.

"My first thought was I wonder what my bail will be and if I could make it so I could still get my methadone the next day," said Bruce, who called his father to post bail and then passed out in the lockup bullpen.

"When I would get a high bail, my dad would never pay them; he'd always make me sit and wait for a reduction," said Bruce, who had put his long-suffering old man through the routine many times. Bail review wouldn't take place until Monday, "and I knew I was going to go into diazepam withdrawal and methadone sickness."

By Monday morning, Bruce was having petit mal seizures along with withdrawal. In the lockup, other suspects were laughing at him: "That dude *sick*."

"I had no strength and barely made it into the courtroom for the bail review," said Bruce. "The judge looked at me, reduced my bail, and sent me back to jail. A few hours later I was called for release."

When one of the administrative officers returned Bruce's belongings, including the drugs he'd had when arrested, "I start shoving Valium in my mouth, and the CO says, 'Stop it. You're not going to die here.'"

Bruce told the guy he was sorry, he was just sick, and, said White, "He gave me that all-knowing nod and went about the business of [processing] release. As I'm walking out I have another seizure and go down in the front yard of the jail.

"I saw my dad's car and forced myself up to get to it, because I wanted to make the methadone program before it closed."

Charles took his son to get his methadone fix, said the T-bird was back on Seminary Avenue and that Robert J. Steinberg had taken the case. Steinberg, the White family attorney who Bruce had come to believe was invincible, beat the rap in court.

Bruce then began sleeping in the family den next to the garage.

11

The Stolen Carpet and the Fat Girl

STATE OF MARYLAND INMATE
NO. 215–799, MARCH 1991
TO AUGUST 1994

"My hustle was just about gone."
—*Bruce White, sinking by degrees*

The first time Bruce White went to prison it was over a small Persian rug in the front hallway of his parents' home. He had moved back to Seminary Avenue—"I was always welcome and comfortable there," he said—after the shootout at Greg Burke's house in Govans.

"I'd wake up each morning and go to the methadone clinic and then go to Lexington Market to buy and sell pills," he said of his daily routine.

He was becoming the kind of addict he'd always looked down on, a guy running out of hustles both clever and audacious, a junkie wandering downtown in search of whatever it took to get high a few times a day. "Any kind of pill to make me not feel like me," he said. The bottom of the barrel was Phenergan, a motion sickness pill that can enhance an opiate high and give hallucinations.

"I ended up doing all these weak hustles like medical assistance prescription scams," said the guy once proud of a résumé that included about twenty-five street stickups and some one hundred pharmacy robberies. "I never saw myself getting to a place of such desperation."

(One savvy pharmacist who refused a bogus scrip told him, "If you're going to try and get away with this, at least spell diazepam right.")

His first stretch in prison occurred after hooking up with another pathetic junkie who wasn't above taking advantage of the White family's hospitality. "At that point," said Bruce, "anybody could be my running buddy if they had a little bit of money."

The running buddy *du jour*—February and March of 1991—was John J. Szymanski, a guy a few years older than Bruce who went by "Jay." Bruce knew him from various methadone programs. They most likely hooked up at the Lexington Market, a Baltimore landmark dating to 1782 and notorious as a hangout for addicts and petty thieves.

"We started hanging out a little bit, eating pills and smoking pot," said Bruce of Szymanski, who lived in Timonium, near the White family home. "We were both guys still living with our families at the ripe age of thirty-something."

On March 8, 1991, "Jay and I went out and got some coke that I paid for," said Bruce. "We'd been drinking methadone all day and eating diazepam. So, we were both good and twisted. I had a nice-size bag of coke and a big bag of weed."

They were hanging out in the room at home that Bruce had taken over after leaving Greg Burke's Woodbourne Avenue apartment. "It was next to the garage; we called it the den."

There they sat, wasted on cocaine, with two of Bruce's handguns on the table in front of him: his Python .357 with the six-inch barrel and a .25 semiautomatic pistol.

"I was always paranoid," he said. "I always wanted access to my guns."

FIGURE 11

The no-honor-among-thieves "friendship" that led to Bruce's first stretch in prison began at Baltimore's Lexington Market and ended outside his parents' house in the suburbs. Photo courtesy of Macon Street Books.

Bruce went upstairs to tell his parents—neither of whom was in particularly good health—that he was going over to Jay's house to spend the night. At the top of the stairs, he looked into his mother's room (where she was watching *Wheel of Fortune* on TV) and waved.

"I felt close to Mom and cared for her, but her alcoholism and abuse of tranquilizers" had created a void, said Bruce, none of which occurred to him until years later.

Then—favored son that he was—Bruce walked into his father's room to say hello. "My father got a big speckled-tooth smile and said hello," said Bruce, remembering that his dad wore dental plates. "I sat down on the bed like I always did, patted him on the stomach, and said, 'What's up, Boss?'"

"There was nowhere in the world I was more comfortable than with my father."

From downstairs, Bruce heard a rustling. When he went to see what was going on, he saw Jay with the carpet from the front hall-way "rolled up under his arm. When he saw me, he dropped it and ran for his car."

Bruce ran and grabbed his .25 handgun, went out a side door, and approached Jay's car as the thief was trying to start it.

"He looked at me with absolute fear and locked the door," said Bruce, who tried to shatter the driver's-side window with the butt of his gun until he realized that Jay had put the car in reverse.

"I took the safety off and started firing rounds into the car," said Bruce. "Jay took off, and I went back inside."

Neither of his parents seemed to have heard the commotion or the shots.

"Bruce didn't shoot him," said his brother Andy, living at home at the time with an addict girlfriend named Annette, now long dead. "He just wanted to make a point."

After the point had been made, it didn't occur to Bruce that a fellow junkie in the game of dope and thieving would call the cops. But, just to be safe, he hid the guns in the rafters of the basement. About an hour later, Baltimore County police officers were at the White home. Bruce hid what drugs he had left under the cushions of the living room couch, answered the door, and allowed the two officers to come inside.

"They asked some questions, and I answered them," said Bruce. "A short time later I left in handcuffs."

White was charged with attempted first-degree murder and a felony handgun violation and held on $100,000 bail. The old routine was engaged: Bruce's father would call family attorney Steinberg (a future judge) and wait for his son's bail to be reduced.

Bruce spent twenty-nine days in lockup at the Towson jail, from where he was driven daily to a methadone clinic and allowed Valium procured via a forged prescription that jail authorities had filled for him. This time, his bail was not reduced, his father did not bail him out, and he was shipped to the Baltimore County Detention Center, where no one was concerned about his pharmaceutical needs.

"Within thirty-six hours at the detention center I was having petit mal seizures from [Xanax] withdrawal and full-blown methadone withdrawal," said Bruce. "They put me on the medical unit, and I was as miserable as anyone on the planet."

He languished there for some three months.

At his court appearance in June 1991, Bruce pleaded guilty to assault with intent to maim and the firearms charge—an open-and-shut conviction had it gone to trial, according to Steinberg.

"Bobby Steinberg had genuine concern for my well-being, even though I had zero," said Bruce of his friend, who retired from the bench in 2014. "More than once he got tired of my act."

Judge Leonard Jacobson (who died in 2005) sentenced White to five years—what inmates call "a pound"—in prison.

"I felt nothing about it," said Bruce, who had a few friends in the courtroom—including Greg Burke—but not his parents. White was escorted out of court by sheriff's deputies and held in a bull-pen before transfer to the Department of Corrections.

"I might have been a little excited about what prison was going to be like," he said, echoing how he felt the night before the first day of middle school years before.

Shackled at the ankles and wrists—with a chain around their waists locked to a bulky metal box that enclosed their handcuffs—the convicts shuffled onto a blue bus taking them to the Maryland Correctional Institution, "the old jail in Hagerstown," established in 1942. On the bus there was small talk about the usual: how long they'd been on the street until this most recent jackpot, what they'd been doing on their last run, how fine their new baby's mama was, how the judge had fucked them, and what a piece-of-shit lawyer they had.

"I just sat back and listened to see who had juice," said Bruce, trying to figure out the pecking order.

In the middle of the night, the convicts were delivered to Castle Grayskull, the name inmates had for the Western Maryland prison. "An extremely intimidating place," said Bruce, who recalled tables bolted into concrete floors and correctional officers who didn't mind working over an inmate to get their point across.

"If you were a white boy and you acted right, you was good" with the virtually all-white prison authorities, said Bruce. "These big white boys had been running the prison for a long time, and they did it with confidence.

"I was the only white guy on a forty-nine-cell tier," said White.

The first thing Bruce did was request a white cellmate, and he got one. He knew a few of his fellow inmates from kicking around the justice system, and they "laughed about our situation. We only had a couple years to do and we'd be going home."

Others would do far more time, and a few were never going home. Out in "the yard"—which Bruce had been hearing about for years, somewhat excited to be there like a kid who'd just made the high school varsity team—Bruce lifted weights and played volleyball and baseball.

He also met tough white guys from a fabled part of Baltimore—Pigtown, once a nineteenth-century enclave of immigrant Irish railroad workers, poor whites originally from the South, and slaughterhouses—which he had never experienced firsthand.

"Guys from Pratt and Monroe were the dominant whites inside the prison," said Bruce of the rough area on the near southwest side of downtown Baltimore, not far from where the Baltimore Ravens NFL team plays ball. "If you didn't live there, the only reason you went was to buy drugs."

At first, Bruce mostly walked around the yard by himself, observing. "I looked to see who was doing what, who might have drugs," he said. "I stayed in the yard as long as I could. I had nothing in my cell, not even a book."

The second bunk in the two-man cell was soon taken by a forty-something-year-old white guy named Bobby, "a true sociopath," said Bruce. Bobby had first gone to prison in 1972, when Bruce was thirteen.

"Goddamn, he was a natural criminal," said Bruce, who towered over his diminutive cellmate and did not fear him. "He came from a family with money in Anne Arundel County, had done a lot of prison time, knew everybody, and wasn't about drugs, just crime. He had an affinity for raping young boys."

Bruce said he found the creep "unpalatable," which is saying something, given the packs White habitually ran in.

As unsavory as Bobby the pedophile may have been, he was key to a hookup that helped Bruce pass the time. Enter the Fat Girl, the roommate of Bobby's girlfriend back home.

"I would be in the yard, and my Fat Girl would be getting out of the car for visiting hours and look over and smile at me," said Bruce. "Guys would joke on me about it—I mean, she must have weighed four hundred pounds—but they all knew she took care of me."

At the end of their face-to-face visits, an inmate and his companion are allowed to kiss. The kisses shared by Bruce and this woman were deep, passionate, filled with longing—and balloons filled with dope.

The Fat Girl—"I don't even remember her name," said Bruce— would hide different-colored balloons filled with narcotics in the recesses of her mouth, transfer the balloons into Bruce's mouth, and continue kissing until White had swallowed them.

"Each balloon had a different substance in it," said Bruce, going down the list from marijuana to heroin and PCP. "She'd bring as much as she could afford or I could get people to give her for me."

As soon as the visit was over, Bruce would return to his cell and vomit the balloons into the sink.

"I would prepare before I went on a visit by drinking about a half gallon of water," he said. "When I got back I would drink another quart with some soap in it, jump up and down, and stick my fingers down my throat until I got the balloons up. If there was something special—like PCP—the balloon would be red."

The PCP was a special treat, a poison cherry on top of a toxic sundae.

"I was so excited to get twisted," said Bruce, his preferred slang for getting high on PCP. "I went up into the shower with two rolled joints of flakes and smoked them. One of the female guards followed me. She used to talk to me when I was alone in the shower and let me jerk off while we talked dirty."

After "the old jail"—where he served most of his time for shooting up Jay's car with Jay in it—Bruce was transferred to the Central Laundry, a minimum-security facility in Sykesville. He did not let his drug-secreting carrier pigeon know about the move and never saw her again.

Maxine and Charles visited their son in the old Hagerstown jail a few times a year in the beginning. Then Maxine had a stroke,

Charles began suffering from Alzheimer's (from which he eventually died), and the visits stopped.

It was at the Central Laundry in Sykesville, a dormitory-style prison where Bruce worked for about a year before his release, that he saw his mother for the first time since her stroke.

"I felt terrible talking to her while she was in a wheelchair and not being able to respond well to the conversation," said Bruce. "My thinking was pretty clear at this point. I had been working out and was looking pretty good. Mom was pleased. But I was still thinking about getting one more hit."

And one more was what Bruce and Greg Burke chased when his old grade school friend picked him up in mid-August of 1994 upon White's release from the custody of the State of Maryland. He'd been imprisoned for forty-four months.

"They gave me twenty dollars and pointed to the door," said Bruce. "I walked out, and there was Greg. He asked me where I wanted to go. I told him I had twenty dollars, let's go get some dope. I did not think about going to see my parents."

At North and Charles, now, as then, one of the main crossroads of Baltimore's junkie community, Bruce said hello to the addicts he hadn't seen for a while. Greg found a dude named Bill who took their money and returned a half hour later to lead them to his nearby apartment at North Avenue and Saint Paul Street. Once there, Greg did something he'd never done before: strongly advised Bruce not to shoot the heroin but snort it.

"For some reason, he didn't want me to use the syringe," said Bruce, and—even stranger—the monkey in charge of White's brain consented.

"After Greg was dead, I found that he'd gotten AIDS in 1992, about two years before I got out of prison," said Bruce. "All I can think is that even a sociopath can have love for a guy he's known since the fourth grade."

And the rug thief?

Said by his family to be depressed and talking about taking his life, Jay Szymanski walked in front of a Light Rail train near his Lutherville home a few days after Memorial Day in 1992. The first pedestrian to be hit by Maryland's Light Rail, Szymanski died not long afterward.

12

Misadventure En Route to the Underworld

1995 THROUGH 1998

> "When it came my turn to get served by the boys selling dope in the alley, the kid said I looked too clean to be an addict. I told him I just got out of Hagerstown after doing three years. He understood and gave me the pills."
>
> —*Bruce, returning to the game*

Within days of his release on supervised probation, on August 17, 1994, Bruce was back to the streets, back to dope, back to robbing people with a gun.

"I knew I could not depend on stealing money from my mother and father to support my habit," he said. "It was time to put in some work."

The work, of course, was dirty—"I didn't have jobs, I did jobs," was one of his favorite mottos—and in a few short years it would become especially ugly.

Back on Seminary Avenue, about four years after her first stroke while Bruce was locked up in Hagerstown, Maxine was found dead in bed while Bruce was getting ready for his daily dose of methadone. Andy, long an addict by now, discovered her cold body. Bruce is convinced that Andy broke their mother's fingers to steal her rings along with other jewelry she was wearing.

"Even at my sickest I wouldn't do something like that," said Bruce, who, after feeling for a pulse and not finding one, "had no feeling about it one way or the other."

It was Bruce who'd given Andy his first shot of heroin—not unlike Fat Donald had injected him years before, leading to decades of depravity for both. There is little or no violence on Andy's record, mostly "petty offenses," according to the attorney who represented both White brothers at various times.

"I'm the first person that stuck a needle in his arm," said Bruce, noting that he and Andy "shot up together" right after he learned that Patti had died. "I've done everything I can to make amends for that," he said. "Nothing I can do about it anymore."

At the time of Maxine's death, her husband Charles was already debilitated by Alzheimer's and unaware that she had passed. Bruce told Andy to call 911 and his mother's attorney, then left to get his methadone.

He and his brothers later attended a memorial service for their mother on the Eastern Shore. Charles did not make the trip.

Maxine was buried near her mother, Mernie.

"She was buried in the same Delaware cemetery as her family," said Bruce. "I got the cold welcome I expected from [Uncle] Butch. I believe that's the last I saw any" of the Johnson family.

> "In a pre-dawn raid on a staid Lutherville street, a Baltimore County police officer yesterday shot and critically wounded a 38-year-old felon suspected of having illegal weapons."
>
> —*Baltimore Sun*

By the first week of January 1998—when a Baltimore County SWAT team swept into the White family home on Seminary Avenue and shot Bruce within a miracle of his life—the rapidly deteriorating

FIGURE 12

Andy White. "I'm the first person that stuck a needle in his arm," said Bruce. "I've done everything I can to make amends for that. Nothing I can do about it anymore." Photo by Jennifer Bishop.

junkie had a ten-year-old daughter he seldom saw, had lost his mother, and was sleeping at night with an automatic rifle.

"Around that time, I'd stay home a lot with my father," said Bruce. "I'd be high on junk, and Dad would have his gin, and we'd sit and watch World War II movies."

On January 7, 1998, he was shot in the den of the home where Maxine once made him happy with spaghetti and meatballs and his other childhood favorite meal, chicken with mushrooms and orange sauce over rice.

From the police department's point of view, the shooting resulted from White's attempted murder of a policeman, tactical officer Brian Cromer. The Baltimore County police investigation synopsis says that officers arrived with a "no knock" warrant on suspicion of firearms violations: a convicted felon in possession of deadly weapons.

Written a day after the shooting, the report states that "continuous announcement" of the officers' presence in the White home was made from the moment they forced their way in at 6 a.m.— through the front door and then into a downstairs bedroom— "very cluttered and dirty," according to police—where Bruce slept.

"Upon forcing the bedroom door . . . Officer Brian Cromer observed the suspect roll from the bed, holding [a] Ruger Mini-14 weapon," read a report written by detectives while Sinai Hospital surgeons were working to save Bruce's life, during which time he had embarked on his journey to the underworld.

"The suspect assumed a kneeling position and began to point the weapon in the direction of the officers. Officer Cromer fired three shots from his service 9mm weapon, striking the suspect in the [stomach, arm,] and leg."

(In late 2020, while White was awaiting replacement of his right knee, doctors found arthritis and bone spurs in that leg. Because

of bullet fragments also there, he cannot undergo magnetic reso-
nance imaging, or MRI. "All very painful," Bruce said. "Who would
have thought I'd get old?" Certainly no one who ever knew him.)

In addition to the gun Bruce was holding when he was shot by
Cromer (the police report identified Cromer as "the victim"), the
raid turned up an M16 rifle, two handguns, lots of ammunition,
and "one bong, black in color with possible residue."

"I'd have shot the fuck out of that motherfucker if I could have,"
said Bruce, who now routinely buys coffee for police officers any-
time they happen to be in the same café together. "I wasn't exactly
a cold-blooded killer, but I would damage people if I had to."

"It was a little bit of a shock," said Woody, though not inconceiv-
able. "My brother has had some problems. As he got older, he was
known to have a few firearms."

Andy was at home during the raid, along with Bruce's father, and
told reporters, "I heard bang, bang, bam, rap, rap, rap. I thought
someone was trying to break into the house." Handcuffed by police
during the incident, Andy said, "I don't think my brother is stupid
enough to point a gun at police officers in riot gear. The only thing
I can think of is he was scared."

After emergency surgery at Sinai Hospital, Bruce was conscious
enough to eavesdrop on the nurses and doctors who had worked
on him. "The bits of their conversations I do remember led me to
believe I was going to die," he said.

Years later, as Bruce recalled the SWAT story at a Baltimore coffee shop, someone in earshot said, "Sounds like a bad day."

"Yeah," replied Bruce. "The next dozen or so years weren't so
great either."

13

Frank White / Inmate Junkie

"BANG! The gavel came down, and that was that."
—*Bruce White, on receiving his sentence*

Any one of a thousand separate moments in the journey of Bruce White—from having his teenage face nearly ripped off in a Christmas car crash to undergoing unneeded surgery simply to get narcotics—would be the worst day in nearly anyone's life.

"Over time, I became truly insane, animalistic really, very comfortable with not showering," he said. "I'd smoke PCP joints for weeks at a time like other people smoke cigarettes. I felt invincible."

But, for the seemingly indestructible White—who still carries a bullet in his left arm below the elbow from the SWAT shooting—life was just starting to get interesting when Judge Christian M. Kahl pounded that gavel in November 1998.

Wild-eyed, wild-haired, enraged, and scary as shit, Bruce began cursing everyone in the room, in particular State's Attorney Jill Pickett and the detective who worked the case.

The most infuriating detail of the case against him, said Bruce, was the insistence of the police that the SWAT team had announced itself before breaking into his bedroom. "That's a lie," he said. "I'm not stupid enough to draw a weapon on the police."

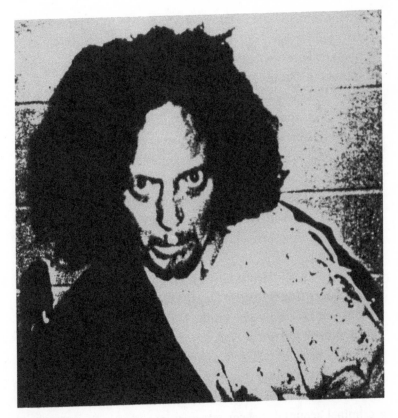

FIGURE 13
Mug shot of Bruce White before his conviction for weapons violations and assault on a police officer in connection with his arrest by a SWAT team in January 1998. Photo courtesy of the Baltimore County Police Department.

In court, "I called the detective a piece of shit and then caught the eye of the cute little blond prosecutor who always dressed so nice. I called her a fucking bitch and everything else in the book. "I could see that no one had ever spoken to her like this. My mouth was the only weapon I had left. She looked scared, and I was enjoying it."

Said the veteran state's attorney of two decades, now married and known as Jill Savage, "Bruce was the scariest guy I ever prosecuted. He reminded me of Charles Manson, with his eyes all bugged out. He seemed to hate everybody with extreme venom."

Bobby Steinberg—Bruce's go-to super-lawyer who had saved the junkie's ass time and time again—finally took a pass. "I refused to represent him any longer. His parents were solid people, and I wasn't going to take their money anymore," said Steinberg, now a retired district court judge for Maryland. "I cared about Bruce, but I couldn't help anymore."

This left Bruce with an attorney recommended by his daughter's maternal grandmother, a lawyer more adept with civil cases than criminal trials.

The attorney, said Bruce, smelled a big-money judgment against the Baltimore County Police Department for unlawfully shooting a civilian in his own home on the basis of a "no knock" warrant. That argument did not prevail.

"I really believe [Officer Cromer] thought Bruce was going to shoot him," said Savage.

And so, instead of filing a wrongful maiming civil case after a criminal acquittal, Bruce's attorney stood by as sheriff's deputies dragged his insane, screaming, bullet-riddled client from the courtroom.

Said Kahl before moving on to his next case, "Have a nice twenty years, Mr. White."

Thus, Mr. White began bouncing around most of the prisons in the state of Maryland on a conviction for first-degree assault on a police officer.

While on the witness stand before his conviction by an all-white jury, Bruce watched as Jill Pickett aimed his Mini-14 rifle around the courtroom, the scope projecting a red-laser bull's-eye wherever she aimed. This, she told the jury, is what the defendant pointed at Baltimore County police officers.

"She said it was the deadliest weapon she'd ever held in her hands," said Bruce. "I looked at the faces of the jury and knew I was in trouble."

In each of the five prisons where Bruce eked out his sentence he found a way to get high. He also learned that you only have two choices when it comes to sleeping: with your head by the toilet, where it stinks, or with your head by the cell bars, where it might be crushed. He chose the toilet.

Bruce began his stretch at the old jail in Hagerstown. Then came the Eastern Correctional Institution in Somerset County on the Eastern Shore, before a transfer to the infamous Maryland House of Correction in Jessup, and finally Western Correctional in Cumberland.

Across those years and miles, he had a single visitor, an attorney named John Van Hoven.

"I was a mean guy, I wasn't the guy you came to see," said Bruce, who wasn't quite so mean that he didn't want to see his own flesh-and-blood. "I bought my daughter a car while I was in prison with money from my father's estate in the hope that she would visit me," he said. "She didn't."

Andy White maintains that he would have visited from time to time if it weren't for Bruce's stipulation: "Don't come unless you bring dope."

Bruce hired Van Hoven for $10,000 to argue for a sentence reduction. He paid a second attorney in Van Hoven's office $10,000 to demand that the state provide treatment for his hepatitis C, which it never did.

Even when on disciplinary segregation or "lockup"—the State of Maryland's version of solitary confinement—Bruce managed

to procure a radio, a fan, a game of Scrabble, and something—
anything—to get high pretty much as often as he wanted.

"I started using drugs just like I did on the street while Van
Hoven worked on my release," said Bruce. "He'd come see me and
say, 'You're high.' I'd remind him I was doing twenty years. What
else was I supposed to do?"

The guards at Jessup, said Bruce, turned a blind eye to most drug
use, as long as there was no violence. Bruce remembered bumping
into a captain at the top of a stairwell early on, and the man said,
""White, you haven't been here twenty-four hours, and your name
is ringing in my ear.'"

Bruce said he had no idea why, and the captain asked if he could
pass a urine test. After lying that his piss was dirty from the last
prison on the Eastern Shore—from which he'd arrived just that
morning—Bruce knew two things: that someone had snitched on
him, and that getting high might be a challenge, but it would not
be a problem.

"At any other prison in the state I would have been tested," he
said. "Sometimes there would be lines in stairwells of people waiting to get served, just like on the corner."

(In other lockups, Bruce was tested often and often failed. Once
in Hagerstown, he got his drug-free cellmate to piss in an empty
bottle of Elmer's glue and—directing a friend to distract a guard
with small talk—switched the clean urine for his own.)

At the House of Correction in Jessup, he said, "drugs flowed like
water. I had no other identity in the joint but a junkie. Every dealer
in prison knew Frank White."

Frank White was the name inmates gave Bruce in his first prison
stint back in 1991. It's the name of Christopher Walken's drug lord
character in the 1990 gangster film *King of New York*. The combo

of Bruce's passing resemblance to Walken and the same last name made the nickname stick.

Years later, when he finally began thinking of himself again as Bruce—an identity he'd long lost touch with—an older woman working in an office told Bruce he reminded her of Clint Eastwood, which made him very happy. But in prison, from one end of the state to the other, he was Frank White.

Frank White to Carlos Murray of the East Baltimore Murray Brothers gang, a longtime tier companion at the old jail in Hagerstown and prison dope buddy, a Jamaican "soldier" in the city's crack cocaine wars of the 1980s.

Frank White to Perry "Rock" Roark, who founded the white prison gang "Dead Man Incorporated" and will likely be behind bars until he dies.

And Frank White to Rudy, the black inmate who washed dishes in the kitchen at Jessup, a highly regarded inmate whose word twice saved Bruce's life.

All three men, said Bruce, respected him, and each, at one time or another, gave him the best surety one can hope for in prison: "I got you, Frank White."

"I had a beef with a guy from Washington who was at the top of the DC food chain," said Bruce. "But in the joint, Rudy was a little bigger."

All Rudy had to do was let the word drop that he and White were friends, and the DC thugs who were after Bruce's dope—and willing to do whatever it took to get it, since he had it hidden in his ass—backed off. To make it clear that Bruce was under his protection, Rudy walked across the prison yard with him for all to see.

Each of those criminals—a Jamaican, a Caucasian, and an African American—swam at the top of the prison food chain. Carlos was a "shark," the other two "whales"—brutal gang dictators. And each was fond of Bruce for no other reason than the way he carried himself—respecting "Frank White" enough to share food and call off predators.

"I wasn't a tough guy, but I wasn't a punk either. I was a stand-up guy that didn't give a fuck," said Bruce. "I would fight you no matter how big you were, and it didn't matter if I got beat up because I had no fucks to give."

This appealed to a guy like Rudy, who revealed himself to Bruce one day in the Jessup kitchen with a simple, almost biblical query: "Don't you know who I am?"

"Yeah," said Bruce with nonchalance. "You're Rudy the dishwasher."

And Rudy chuckled, a genuine laugh that affirmed how much he liked the white junkie the black dudes called Frank White.

> "I saw people step over a dead body to get to lunch."
>
> —*Bruce White*

As the bus of shackled inmates pulled up to the Maryland House of Correction, the notorious late nineteenth-century, eight-hundred-acre prison straddling Anne Arundel and Howard Counties, Bruce had a feeling that things were going to change for him, though he didn't know how.

"In prison, you always talked about how good we'd had it on the street before you got busted," said Bruce. "It was all lies."

The notorious glamour of the Jessup appealed to Bruce. It was a haunted, blood-soaked place of mythical and brutal danger, the last stop for those who would never be set free—"old men in wheelchairs dying of cancer," he said—and criminal graduate school for those who were able to get out.

He spent about a year and a half there in the months following the 9/11 attack on the World Trade Center.

"I thought I was used to prison living. But the Cut showed me that I wasn't."

"The House" to some, Jessup was commonly known as "the Cut" because it was built on forestland shoveled out by hand in the late nineteenth century for the B&O Railroad. The added meaning—a place where you could be stabbed to death without notice—added to the allure.

"Violence was not an everyday occurrence, but it was a weekly one," said Bruce. "I saw life sold cheap and came to respect the pecking order."

Jessup first held inmates about a decade after the end of the Civil War and was the scene of inmate riots in 1945, 1964, and 1972. Those disturbances are just the major recorded outbreaks. Less violent scuffles, along with protests for better living conditions and prison wages—Bruce said he made eighty-five cents a day working the kitchen—were frequent.

Stately and solemn, the Italianate brick edifice could have passed for a midwestern university had the population not been rapists, drug kingpins, and killers locked in six-foot-by-nine-foot cells made of cinderblock and iron. Shut down in March 2007—a year after a correctional officer named David W. McGuinn was stabbed to death and another seriously wounded—the prison was demolished in 2014 with the help of inmate labor.

Though many guards had been assaulted by inmates at the Cut in its long history, McGuinn was the only one murdered, according to Gary N. Hornbaker, the warden at the House of Correction when it closed. Hornbaker, who wasn't in charge during Bruce White's stay, could not say exactly how many inmates had been murdered by other inmates.

"It was an antiquated facility with a lot of blind spots that made security very difficult," said Hornbaker. "We closed it after Officer McGuinn was killed."

When the end came, all but about 850 inmates had been transferred to other prisons. When Bruce arrived, the maximum-security penal colony was still running at the max—upward of two thousand inmates overall, with many of the four-story tiers holding two to a cell.

Bruce waited for his cell assignment in a grand and sordid "center hall"—a soaring atrium where you could look up and see all four tiers stacked upon each other. Inmates who knew him began yelling his name, shouting out gossip—"Yo, I heard so-and-so got killed"—along with the phrase that was sometimes sincere and other times pure bullshit: "I got you, dawg."

"The first thing I did in any prison was observe the social interactions; it tells you more than what is actually being said or done," he said. "You learn the power structure much differently than if you just look for the apex predators."

In the daytime at a prison, you watched—in the yard, in the mess hall. And you most certainly kept the eyes in the back of your head fully open in the dorms and showers. At night you listened. It was virtually never quiet, and there was rarely peace.

"I'd stretch out on my bunk and listen to people yelling up and down the tiers to one another, shouting about wanting a pack of instant noodles or some Little Debbie [lunch cakes] or how much they were going to lift in the yard the next day," said Bruce, noting that incessant chatter characterized every prison where he served time.

"Then you'd have a guy explaining an entire TV show to the guy a couple cells down, going into detail about how the characters were dressed and what the sets looked like."

All of which you had to accept—along with occurrences like the murder Bruce witnessed in the cage next to him around the time of his forty-second birthday—or go out of your mind.

"I was on [segregated] lockup and looked out my small window and heard two cellmates arguing. It doesn't take a lot to get in an argument with your cell buddy in a tiny lockup," said Bruce.

The argument was about a light: one guy said turn it off, and the other did not heed the request. After a scuffle, the man who had to repeat his request that the light be turned off yelled out, "I murdered this motherfucker!"

Shortly, guards went into the cell, handcuffed the blood-splattered survivor, and took him away.

"Funny thing is," said Bruce, "the dead guy was serving ninety-six years and was never going to get out. The guy who killed him was scheduled to be released in a few months."

Sometimes, he said, you'd have a hunch who is going to become unhinged and kill themselves or someone else. Sometimes it came as a surprise.

"There's always outliers wherever you are. In prison you don't want to know them or have them know you," said Bruce. "I had no illusion that these people were my friends." Yet he cultivated relationships of relative trust and nurtured a slight hope—like an oven whose pilot light is all but out but flickers dimly—that something good might come of the experience.

"I sensed that things could get very bad at the Cut," he said, remembering how it felt when the bus passed through the gates. "But something else told me that maybe there'd be some good to come out of it too."

Both poles would hold true as his sentence played out, including seeing a desperately frightened inmate trembling on his bunk just before two other men dragged him into the shower and stabbed him to death. Afterward, Bruce said, the killers calmly sat down on a dormitory bunk not far from where the dead man once slept and shared the kind of lunch cakes that kids eat at school.

"I thought to myself—this is where I ended up," said Bruce, who at times worried that a victory at chess could lead to death. "In a place where you walk up to someone and murder them, then go back and eat dessert as if nothing had happened."

The Mountains of Western Maryland: Razor Fights and a Familiar Hospital

> "If you gave me eight thousand sounds to choose from, I could tell you right away which one was a prison door locking shut. It's very distinct, and by the three-thousandth time you've heard it, it's almost comforting. It means you're safe for the night."
>
> —*Bruce, at home in institutions*

About fifteen years after his wife died on the back of his motorcycle in Western Maryland, Bruce again found himself at Washington County Hospital in Hagerstown where he was taken after the Labor Day weekend 1984 crash that took Patti White's life.

"It brought back so many memories," said Bruce, "and made me think again what a mess my life had become."

It was the winter months of 1999, and he was early in his stretch at the Maryland Correctional Institution, the "old jail" in Hagerstown. A heroin overdose had sent him to the hospital, where he arrived with several slowly healing razor wounds over his left eye, the result of a "shank fight" over dope.

The beef: Bruce had dope, and the inmate in the next cell wanted some. When Bruce refused to share, the other guy "told me he would see me in the shower, so I prepared myself," fashioning a spike with a soda can and a ballpoint pen.

"I took a soda can and ripped it open and wrapped the aluminum around the ends of the pen. Then I used the heel of my slipper to bang the metal around the points at each end."

Now armed, he entered the shower with his antagonist, the guard locked them in, and they squared off.

"When I was alone with the guy he said, 'Frank White, how you want it?' Before he finished talking, I attacked with my shank. He hit me a few times with a toothbrush that had a razor blade melted into it.

"We were both bleeding, and I had a good-size gash beside my eye. The guard came, and I acted like I was drying my face, and the other guy pretended to dry his body. We went back to our cells and patched ourselves up. I never had a problem with him again."

Soon, Bruce went to the medical unit to have the wound treated. He said he'd cut himself while exercising. Whether they believed him or not was not discussed. And then he overdosed on "good mud heroin, brown shit from Mexico," of which he had squirreled away about twenty-five dollars' worth.

When he was released from the hospital the next day, jail officials had him pee in a cup, and it came back dirty.

"If I remember correctly," said Bruce, "they gave me 485 days in lockup, most of it because they found out about the fight in the shower. Sooner or later, the guards find out everything."

After ten months in segregation—"you do ten months locked in a bathroom and you'd have enough too," said Bruce—they let him back in the general population. "Who knows why? They just did."

While Bruce was being shifted among institutions on the whim of wardens and bureaucrats and sent to lockup for drug-related infractions, the guy who gave him his first shot of heroin—and helped save his ass in Harlem years before—died.

"Fat Donald" Eckert, said Bruce, was either murdered or overdosed. His death notice stated that Donald E. Eckert died "suddenly," on February 11, 1999.

"Donald had to be murdered, that's what everybody said. He'd been shooting dope for too long to overdose. Maybe today with fentanyl he might OD, but not back then."

The World Trade Center towers came down as Bruce snorted heroin at the Cut. When the space shuttle Columbia exploded on reentry the first day of February 2003, Bruce was smoking marijuana laced with PCP.

"Being in prison when stuff like that happens just makes you feel more separated from the world," he said.

And, back in 2000, about two years into his sentence, Bruce lost his one, true best friend with the death of his eighty-three-year-old father, Charles Wood White Sr., born June 13, 1917.

"I got a letter from my father's insurance company that I would be getting $10,000, and later that month I received a checkbook so I could spend it," said Bruce. "I couldn't believe the checkbook made it past the mailroom. It went real fast on drugs and lawyers."

The authorities couldn't keep him from the inheritance, but they refused to escort him to his father's funeral.

"I had made everything good with my father before I even went to trial," said Bruce. "I told him I loved him."

Dad's money allowed him to buy just about whatever he wanted in prison, from heroin to special food from the commissary. Anything other than bland prison rations—"it sucks," said Bruce—had to be paid for in cash, trade, or favors: cans of tuna, instant noodles, and the Little Debbie lunch cakes favored by men who stab other men to death in the communal shower.

On his steady, four-decade swirl down the societal drain, Bruce experienced a number of moments best described as "How did it come to this?"

None made much of an impression. Bruce would simply shake off any uncomfortable truth for another hit of something to forget himself for a few hours—and thus would slip another rung or two down the ladder of madness.

These reckonings were rooted in childhood recklessness—if one kid was going to ride his bike off a ten-foot hill, Bruce would fly off a twenty-foot hill to show who was the alpha male of eleven-year-olds.

Soon, drugs would fuel greater danger while becoming close to fatal for Bruce and those in his orbit. Sometime in 1982 or 1983, Brue and his future wife Patti were buying pounds of PCP at a time for sale and personal use.

"Sometimes I would stay up for days on end," he said. "I got so whacked, I thought the radio was sending me messages. I was so saturated with PCP that I was intoxicated even when I wasn't smoking it.

"One day, the music on the radio told me that everyone in the house was evil and it was my job to cleanse it," said Bruce, who was living at home with Patti on Seminary Avenue at the time. He grabbed the Mini-14 he so loved, the one that would factor in his getting shot by the police and sent to prison a few years later.

As Bruce loaded a round, Patti asked what he was doing, and he told her: the radio said I have to cleanse the house of evil.

Patti ran screaming from the bedroom and down the stairs. Bruce walked around "like I was dreaming" while holding a semi-automatic rifle out in front of him—on alert like a grunt moving through the jungle—as his mother came around the corner.

Maxine demanded, "What the hell do you think you're doing?"

And in that moment, said Bruce, "I took a good look at her, and I knew she was a good person and I was insane." Setting the rifle against the wall, Bruce took off all his clothes, took three ounces of PCP from the freezer in his parents' garage, sat down cross-legged in the driveway, and dumped the chemical-laced parsley flakes over his body.

"Next thing I know," said Bruce, "I'm strapped down in an ambulance."

Now, in drug-addled, incarcerated middle age, Bruce had lost his pride in one of his main areas of self-esteem: the ability to be a successful criminal. No longer was he the rakish masked man who could stick a gun in a pharmacist's face and demand drugs as casually as other people ordered cheeseburgers at a drive-through.

In prison, a cheap radio, an electric fan, and a board game were luxuries. And dope no longer provided escape from the skin in which he'd been born.

"My life had come down to living in a small, locked room and getting high," he said. "And even when I was high I was still in misery. I had to be completely nodded out to have any peace."

Suicide "never crossed my mind," said Bruce, figuring that dope or the life of a guy who needed dope around the clock would likely bring the end. But maybe, just maybe, he might get clean for the first time since he was an eleven-year-old kid smoking pot, drinking liquor, and riding his minibike.

In the past, any talk of someone getting clean—especially if it was a female addict he was involved with—made him extremely anxious. "I lived in a world where I didn't know anybody who was clean," said Bruce. "Everybody I knew was either getting high, on methadone, in prison, or dead."

The road to becoming a guy who didn't use drugs began one day in the Jessup "annex" near the main prison. Bruce was preparing to shoot up after the guard on duty passed by during a head count.

"I got my syringe and cooker and hung the curtain in my window as if I was taking a crap; I loved the whole ritual of it"—and jammed the needle as he had done thousands of times before.

"I drifted in and out of a nod for hours, and when I woke up and looked at myself in the little hubcap of a mirror, I knew I was just as miserable high as I was straight."

He flushed the syringe down the toilet and, recalling a line from the prison movie *The Shawshank Redemption*, decided it was time to "get busy living or get busy dying."

Though he chose living (or, maybe he had nothing to do with it), the moment he "kicked dope" wouldn't be the last time he used illegal drugs.

"But it was the catalyst," he said. "I knew I was done."

The last time Bruce stuck a needle in whatever vein he had left came about a month later, sometime in mid-June of 2003. He eventually chose his wife Patti's birthday (June 19) as his clean date. Bruce was at WCI, the Cumberland prison that replaced the Cut.

"You had to walk about a quarter mile to the chow hall, but I enjoyed looking at the mountains," said Bruce, noting that WCI had tighter security than his previous prisons but offered more recreation.

At the time, he was sharing a cell with a prison drug dealer named Kareem, "a very dangerous young man with a look in his eye that I've never seen in any other human being." It was while he was locked up with this madman—a guy who might have a fit or attack you if he lost at chess—that Bruce shot dope for the last time. Kareem didn't use drugs; he sold them for money and status in prison.

One day, after deciding to get clean, Bruce observed Kareem cutting dope into small bags. He asked Bruce if he wanted any.

"Without a thought I said yes," said Bruce. "As soon as it was in my hand I knew the answer was supposed to be no. But I couldn't tell him I'd made a mistake."

This led to getting high—or as close to it as he could get, since dope was no longer providing escape—for the next two weeks. Arguments with Kareem over debts for dope amplified Bruce's desire to quit.

(Kareem did not understand, or care to, that Bruce was paying with money that had to be forwarded to the prison by his stockbroker and that this took more time than a cash handoff on the corner. Then again, it's unlikely Kareem had ever sold dope to an inmate with a stockbroker.)

"All I had ever been was a junkie—what else could I possibly be?" he said of this turning point. "In my soul, I knew I had to live clean."

The last time Bruce shot dope—forty-four years old and utterly miserable—was so unmemorable that he has nothing memorable to say about it.

"I just stopped using," he said, decades down the road from his first shot in the backseat of his beloved Super Bee, the hot rod that had carried him into the dark and haunted parking lots of the underworld.

Weight-lifting and exercise—"positive addictions," said Bruce—filled the void. A little more than two years later, he was out—free of the Maryland Department of Corrections, if not himself.

"When Judge Kahl released me on October 20, 2005, he said, 'You are free to go home,'" remembered Bruce. "And even though I was happy, I was freaked out because I didn't have a home to go to."

So, what about Rudy, the middle-aged dishwasher who turned out to be the whale who ran the notorious Black Guerrilla Family gang at the Cut, the guy who interceded on Bruce's behalf with badass inmates from the District of Columbia who wanted Frank White dead over a mundane drug beef?

The last Bruce heard, Rudy was out of the joint and hanging around the Lexington Market, back in the game that had sent him to prison so many times before.

And Rock, the guy who called Bruce "Pop" with affection?

Sentenced to life in prison at age forty-three in 2013 on racketeering charges, the predator proclaimed at his guilty plea that Dead Man Incorporated no longer represents who he is.

Carlos?

"Who the fuck knows?" said Bruce.

And, most especially, what about Frank White?

"I have nothing in common with any of them," said Bruce. "But a fucked-up past."

14

Free to Go

"As I tried to talk, tears started rolling down my eyes."
—*Bruce White*

The self-described animal who would do anything necessary to get what he needed to stay high had been drug-free behind bars for a little more than two years.

"My mind was beginning to clear, and my spirit had something I hadn't noticed before—hope," said Bruce, who replaced heroin with lifting weights in the prison yard. "Maybe I could make something out of myself.

"You'd think after being shot, stabbed, having contracts put out on me, and my wife dying because of my addiction that I would have quit using long ago—but it wasn't until I was in a maximum-security prison that I came face to face with myself for the first time."

As when—face to face with the judge who had sent him to prison nearly a decade earlier—sincere tears of remorse fell from his eyes.

It was October 20, 2005, in the Towson Courthouse before Judge Christian Kahl, the man who had wished Bruce "a good twenty years" back in '98. At a previous hearing, the judge had cut five years from White's sentence and was about to pass judgment again.

FIGURE 14
Bruce revisits the North Avenue Motel where he stayed in the first weeks after his release from prison. Photo by Jennifer Bishop.

"I felt like the boy who'd been molested and couldn't tell anybody," remembered Bruce. "Like the fourteen-year-old who acted out all the time because of fear, the guy who killed his wife and unborn child." All rumbling inside the beaten convict as Bruce leaned on the "court cane," a prop to elicit sympathy; a toxic mix of un-anesthetized shame, guilt, and fear, none of which Bruce had addressed while staying high for two-thirds of his life.

Unable to put words to it, "I held up my arms in front of the judge in surrender, with tears on the front of my prison shirt," said Bruce. "Death would have been a relief."

To which Judge Kahl—a man remembered upon his death in 2016 as "kind and patient"—said, "I don't feel that Mr. White is a threat to anyone anymore. I will let him go home."

The conditions: establish a residence in thirty days, a year of home detention, and three years' probation. The home detention part would be tricky in that the forty-six-year-old had nowhere to go. His parents were dead, and the family home had been sold by his mother's attorney, the proceeds divided between Bruce and his brothers. Brother Andy was in the wind, using dope, living day to day.

Years later, still struggling to get by, Andy would join the chorus of people surprised that Bruce was aboveground, saying, "I was surprised he was still alive when he was eighteen."

And Woody—who Bruce said sold his cars while he was in prison (an '89 Lincoln Continental and the turbo '84 T-Bird)—was the brother who volunteered to testify against brother in the trial that sent Bruce away.

"When I hit the streets after being in the joint all those years, all I had was my story, nothing else," said Bruce.

Just his story and, a moment later, five bucks from a stranger who came up to say that he'd just witnessed what went down before Judge Kahl.

"The guy said, 'I can't believe what just happened to you,' and gave me five dollars," said Bruce. "He said I was going to need it."

Now he had his story and bus fare. Out in the world as a free man for the first time in nearly a decade (sans cane), Bruce wasn't thinking of contacting his siblings or visiting his parents' graves. He was simply pumped with adrenaline from this startling thing that had just happened to him, excitement that he has come to identify as fear.

Fear pushed him down Bosley Avenue toward a York Road bus stop, a blue Department of Corrections shirt with DOC stenciled on it still on his back. He was headed to the place he knew best—downtown Baltimore, where the junkies congregated.

When the bus came, Bruce asked the driver for a transfer, not re-alizing that the system had done away with transfers while he was away—"We haven't used them in years," the driver told him—and now sold day passes.

Which got him to the corner of Greenmount and North Av-enues near Baltimore's fabled Green Mount Cemetery, final rest-ing place of Baltimore library founder Enoch Pratt, Johns Hopkins of university and hospital fame, and the arch-villain John Wilkes Booth, along with some sixty-five thousand others.

"I was optimistic, but I was very concerned about my future on the street," said Bruce. "I didn't even have the number of someone to call."

A half dozen blocks to the west was the intersection of North Avenue and Charles Street, to this day notorious for its constant gaggle of junkies, methadone addicts, criminals both petty and dangerous, and beggars trying to get something to eat between shots of dope. He would make his way there, a homeless man with-out identification walking the streets in a prison shirt. But first—a candy bar!

"I wanted a Zagnut bar; I hadn't had one in years," said Bruce, who crossed to the south side of North Avenue and into a Rite-Aid in search of a goodie he and Greg Burke (whose funeral Bruce had attended not long before going to prison) enjoyed to-gether as kids.

Scanning the candy shelves, he was paralyzed by the seemingly endless amount of choices. He had enough money left from the five bucks and the bus ride to make one selection. While reaching for a Zagnut, "I saw Pom-Poms and picked them up," he said. "Then I saw Junior Mints and wanted them, so I put the Pom-Poms down. Then I wanted something else, and I just put it all back."

Heart racing, anxious about the fact that he couldn't make a simple choice, Bruce left the store, realizing just how institutionalized he'd become.

"After years of having my meals slopped on a tray and slid toward me, I couldn't even buy a candy bar," he said. "The fear I felt that first day on the street was stronger than any I experienced in prison."

Heading west on North Avenue toward downtown, he stopped at the McDonald's just off the corner of Charles Street, the fast-food joint where addicts routinely request nine to ten sugars with a small coffee.

"I was uneasy with freedom and needed something familiar," he said. "I'd spent many years around there and immediately saw people I knew, many standing like the half-bent-over grotesque statues methadone addiction turns people into."

As he passed with a combination of disdain and sympathy, he was sure that someone would call out, "What's up, Bruce?" Knowing he was a junkie, they'd ask him what he wanted.

"None of them had any idea that I'd been away, they were all living Groundhog Day," he said. "Everybody I knew was in prison, dead, or on methadone."

Bruce got a small coffee and began walking to John Van Hoven's law office about twenty blocks south, near the harbor. Van Hoven gave him about $500 in cash while the attorney's secretary set about getting copies of Bruce's vital records.

A few days later, the prison forwarded Bruce's meager belongings to Van Hoven's office, none of it worth more than a couple of bucks on the street, said Bruce, but important to him—a $189 TV, some clothes, and photographs.

Walking back to the North Avenue McDonald's to get a bite, he ran into an old methadone friend from Sheppard Pratt named

Carey Davis, a guy a little older than himself who breathed with a 24/7 oxygen tank while chain smoking.

"I don't know how he didn't blow himself up," said Bruce. "But Carey helped me out a lot, driving to get things I needed. I would give him gas money or buy him something to eat, but he never asked for anything."

While Carey couldn't save himself—never kicking dope or methadone and eventually dying of complications related to emphysema—he was heaven-sent to Bruce at the end of October 2005. As the days wore on, the angels kept coming.

That night, Bruce got a sixty-eight-dollar room across North Avenue from the McDonald's, purchased the services of a prostitute, and remained at the motel for the next month to comply with Judge Kahl's order that he establish a residence within thirty days of release.

It was at North Avenue and Howard Street, a few blocks from the hamburger joint, that for the first time in a decade Bruce saw his daughter, age ten when he was sent away and now a young woman of seventeen. Nikki and her grandmother arrived by car.

"I was living in the motel and wanted to see her, so I walked down to the corner and waited," said Bruce. "They pulled up, and we went to lunch."

On that afternoon, Bruce's relationship with his only child began anew.

"I very much wanted to know this beautiful young girl, everything about her," said Bruce. "What I didn't know was all the damage that had been done since I was away. She has the same addiction that I do, the same hard-headedness."

Their relationship has proven to be among the most difficult and heartbreaking of his life—White called it "one of the saddest parts of my existence." The struggle to help Nikki find a better way of life continued into late 2020.

"I help people get clean," said Bruce of a primary pillar of his recovery. "And I can't help the one closest to me."

He has paid for her to go into drug treatment facilities in Maryland and Florida. And at least twice, he said, Nikki has lived in one of the "recovery houses" he operates for addicts attempting to get clean. And twice he has had to ask her to leave.

But during Halloween week in 2005, Nikki was still a high school kid trying to figure out the way forward. After lunch, Diane dropped Bruce back at his fleabag, the best he could manage at the time.

"No one was opening their door for me and saying, 'Stay here,' and I'm not the kind of guy to ask," said Bruce. "So, I got a room. It was a dank little spot used by prostitutes and addicts. I felt very comfortable there."

The nineteen-year-old hooker had asked Bruce if he wanted company as he was crossing North Avenue to his room. He said yes and then asked how much. She said thirty dollars, and off they went.

"I could feel an erection starting before we got to the door," said Bruce. "As I sat on the bed watching her undress, I couldn't believe the last twenty-four hours of my life."

The young woman, Bruce said, seemed to understand his situation and was gentle with him, providing more than he'd paid for, thanking him and leaving.

"When she left I took a shower and thought how lonely it was to shower alone, without all the joking and carrying on," he said, surprised that he missed the camaraderie of prison showers.

Day Two in the real world: Bruce woke up, did some push-ups and calisthenics, and grabbed an Egg McMuffin across the street before catching the bus to Towson. There, he went to his father's brokerage house and got a few checks from what was left of his inheritance—three or four, amounting to about $2,500—with no way to cash them. Eventually, on Carey's word, someone took the chance.

Back at North and Charles, the leaning statues of broken humans continued to call to Bruce, knowing him as a fellow traveler.

"What's up?" became "Wanna get high?"

The day before, clean since the nineteenth of June, 2003, Bruce had answered without reservation, "I don't get high anymore."

Now, it was, "I'm *trying* not to get high anymore."

The difference—small but profound—rattled him. He knew he was in trouble and went looking for help, not knowing a soul who had recovered from the progressive and fatal disease of addiction.

"I tried the Man Alive methadone clinic around the corner on Maryland Avenue, hoping they could tell me where to find a Narcotics Anonymous meeting," said Bruce, who knew next to nothing about twelve-step recovery programs. "I was fighting the urge to use," he said. "I knew it was the only hope this old junkie had left."

Hope dissipated when someone at the Man Alive reception desk said they had no information regarding NA meetings but could sign Bruce up for their methadone program. He well knew methadone as no more than another addiction and passed on the offer.

As he walked out, a barely conscious young woman in a diazepam nod on a lobby bench—"she couldn't have been more than eighteen or nineteen," said Bruce—called out to him. He remembers her reaching into her shopping bag—one he said was lined with tin-foil to deflect shoplifting detectors—and handing him a crumpled piece of paper listing local NA meetings.

"I don't know why the fuck I have this," he recalls her saying. "You can have it."

"That list," said Bruce, "saved my life."

Not long before voluntarily attending his first meeting of recovery (he'd been to one in prison before, just to get out of his cell), Bruce treated himself to a box of fast-food fried chicken near his motel.

"It was so good, you would have thought it was filet mignon and lobster tail after years of bland prison food," he said, remembering that—just like Colonel Sanders promises—he licked his lips *and* his fingers.

At 8 p.m. on the day the semiconscious junkie gave him the meeting directory, Bruce arrived at Maryland Avenue and Twenty-Sixth Street, seven blocks from his room, for the New Hope meeting of Narcotics Anonymous at the Weisman-Kaplan House, a satellite facility of Baltimore's pioneering Tuerk House treatment center originally established in 1969 for alcoholics. It now served addicts as well.

At his first meeting there, his second day out of prison, Bruce didn't know anyone in the room. And he felt very anxious.

"I walked down some steps into a dank, smelly basement," he said. "There was a long cafeteria table with coffee, and I made myself a cup and went further into the room. I saw a large table with chairs around it and old broken-down chairs and couches around the edges of the room. A man came up and introduced himself as Derek, saw I was in a prison uniform, and gave me a hug. That made me very uncomfortable, but deep down it felt good. He told me to grab a seat and relax.

"Another guy came in the room talking and stood right behind my chair. This made me extremely uneasy—just yesterday I was in maximum-security prison, and I was very anxious. I had to get up and sit with my back against a wall.

"Then Derek introduced the guy sitting next to him, and the guy began to tell his story. He started talking about his childhood, then his early drug use, from how it was fun for a while and then it was depraved. He said he'd been clean for eighteen months, and his life had never been better.

"He talked about having a sponsor. I had no idea what that was, but I knew this: Here was a hard-core addict that did anything to get one more, and for eighteen months he had not found it necessary to get one more. He spoke from the heart with honesty."

When Derek asked the room if there was anyone who wanted to introduce himself, Bruce raised his hand and said, "I'm an addict named Bruce."

No longer was he Frank White, prison junkie. He was Bruce White, recovering addict.

He left the meeting sweating from anxiety but somehow at peace. He wanted to go to another meeting. Bruce had come home.

"I walked home that night and felt like things might change," he said. "The next day I bought a sweatshirt so I had something to put over my prison shirt."

"I found redemption in that meeting," said Bruce. "I had been real, real broken for a long time."

He began attending NA regularly, often more than one meeting a day, and in about a month moved into 2101 Maryland Avenue, five blocks from the New Hope group.

"I guess it cost about $1,000 a month for utilities and everything," said Bruce, noting that what was left of his inheritance was enough to live on modestly for about a year.

"I would have stayed there forever because I didn't know what else to do," he said. "One of the first nights I was sleeping on the floor, and a mouse bit me on my thumb. I chased him into the bathroom and killed him."

Bruce's daughter Nikki helped him pick out furniture. Although positive change in him was evident, his violence was not exclusive to rodents, as an appliance store salesman found out when Bruce tried to buy a couple of televisions with money orders.

"One guy said that they'd accept money orders, so that's what I got. The next day this other guy says they can't accept them," said Bruce. "I wound up cussing and threatening him."

The sales clerk did not relent, and Bruce used the money orders to buy TVs from a competitor.

But fancy new TV sets and a good mattress—things Bruce had taken for granted growing up, along with new cars, family vacations, and good meals—wouldn't make a dent in his disease.

15

Third Time a Charm

"I thought recovery was finding something that you had lost. But what kind of life had I ever really had to begin with? How do you recover something you never had?"

—*Bruce White*

The first time Bruce White encountered Narcotics Anonymous was in the late 1980s when he met someone outside a meeting in Pikesville to cop dope. His hookup was at NA to get a slip signed proving he was going to court-ordered meetings.

"The guy told me to wait and he'd take care of me when the meeting was over, but I was dope sick and drove to where the meeting was," said Bruce, who said that he openly mocked people who went to twelve-step meetings.

"After I got my drugs, I left and never saw that guy again."

The second time he crossed paths with NA was in prison for his 1998 conviction on weapons charges.

Shortly after landing at the old jail in Hagerstown, Bruce lit up a joint of reefer before heading out to the prison yard and offering a hit to a younger inmate named Marc S., a guy with a light sentence, whom Bruce had given permission to hang in his cell to watch television. Marc declined the reefer, saying he was clean and a member of Narcotics Anonymous. Bruce laughed and kept sucking on the joint.

"I wasn't exactly sure what he was talking about when he said NA, but I didn't care," said Bruce. "I'd seen guys go to these 'meetings' and thought they just wanted to look good at their next parole hearing. If you asked me, I'd have said they were weak."

Some eight years later, Bruce White found himself sobbing in front of the judge who'd sent him away, too weak to describe how pitiful his life had become.

His third rendezvous with Narcotics Anonymous occurred when the woman in the lobby of the methadone clinic gave him the NA directory.

The power of recovery, Bruce would learn, is in the word "can." It is accepted wisdom that genuine sobriety—abstinence from mind-altering substances accompanied by contentment—is not for those who *need* it. If that were true, a city sinking beneath an epidemic of drug abuse and its attendant crime—a city like Baltimore, where heroin has crippled generations since the Great Depression—would be transformed overnight. Rather, recovery can be had by people who *want* it, and Bruce—by this time forty-six years old with nothing to his credit but a life of crime, violence, and sorrow—wanted it badly.

He regularly attended the Wednesday night New Hope meeting near his apartment on Maryland Avenue, but his manner—a guy with a short fuse who at times acted as though he was still in prison—was off-putting, even to other addicts. Many people in the group avoided Bruce, making it difficult for him to find someone willing to "sponsor" him—a person with quality clean time to guide him through NA's twelve spiritual exercises known around the world as "the steps." (Established in 1939 by Alcoholics Anonymous, the twelve steps are the basic principles of recovery upon which NA and many other recovery programs are based.)

FIGURE 15
The Weisman-Kaplan House, a recovery residence where Bruce attended his first
NA meeting, October 21, 2005. Photo by Jennifer Bishop.

"I shoved a couple guys at meetings when I didn't like what they said," said Bruce. "Usually it had to do with my twisted sense of 'respect' that I carried from prison."

One night, he heard a guy named Wesley tell his story at a meeting—"this guy really believed in what he was saying," said Bruce.

Bruce still couldn't bring himself to ask anyone to formally sponsor him. Sensing this, Wesley volunteered. In their ten months working the steps of NA together, Wesley helped Bruce with the first three, which are designed to bring addicts to surrender to both their disease and a power greater than themselves, whatever they decide that might or might not be.

For all of the fear and belligerence that remained in him, Bruce was changing. Before long he'd be saying things like, "I don't care what God anybody has. I just want them to have a God."

At first, those who knew him from prison called him "Boot," in reference to the special, heavy-soled shoe he wears on his damaged right leg. But soon he was simply "Bruce," another addict—though a colorful one—on the road to recovery.

Into the great void that opened when he stopped chasing and using drugs no matter the cost, he brought willingness. That willingness attracted spirits like an auto mechanic Bruce had known years before named Steve Sturgis.

Carey Davis, the chain-smoking methadone addict who had helped Bruce out with everything from rides to vouching for him to get checks cashed to helping secure the apartment on Maryland Avenue, mentioned to Bruce that their old friend Sturgis was clean and doing well.

Sturgis owned a mechanic shop and used-car lot called Atlas Auto at 4420 York Road, just a couple of miles from Ready Avenue where Bruce had the shootout some twenty years earlier when he tried to trade a TV for dope. One day, Carey took Bruce over to see the fruits of recovery on display.

When they arrived, Steve's brother Butch, who recognized Bruce, was getting out of a tow truck. Walking his old friend into the office, Butch told Steve—neither of whom had seen Bruce in twenty-five years—"Look what I found in the parking lot!"

(Harry "Butch" Sturgis IV was never able to hold on to recovery for long and died in December 2015 from an overdose.)

Bruce told Steve that he'd been clean for more than two years, and Steve replied, "Well then, we need to go to a meeting."

Soon, Bruce was working at Atlas. Though he wasn't looking to hire anyone, Steve created a position for Bruce based on little more than one man helping another.

Bruce's legit résumé included teenage dishwasher, a brief stint as a carpet installer, a go-fer at a hotel, and a bouncer at Baltimore's storied No Fish Today blues club, a Eutaw Street landmark that had hosted J. B. Hutto, James Cotton, and Clarence "Gatemouth" Brown over the years before it was destroyed by arson in 1982. His other jobs included pharmacy robberies, interstate drug dealing, and serving chow in prison.

"I hadn't put in any job applications because my self-esteem was so low and I only had eight teeth in my mouth. I couldn't imagine anyone would want me," said Bruce. "Steve gave me an '84 Harley-Davidson that I could ride to work and meetings and had a friend file paperwork so I could get my license back.

"But the thing he gave me that I really needed was his time. He took an interest in me."

A few weeks after he was hired, Bruce began changing oil and brakes and doing other simple maintenance.

"You wouldn't call me a mechanic, but I was a good parts re-placer," said Bruce. "I'd clean up and make sure everything was in proper order at the end of the night. I'd work until about 6 p.m., and most nights Steve and I would hit a meeting."

Not long after that, he was running the office while the real mechanics fixed automobiles.

"I took care of all the bills and payroll, making sure all of the clients were happy," said Bruce. "One guy told Steve I was great, but I needed to get some teeth in my mouth."

Bruce became a patient at the University of Maryland Dental School downtown, and Steve was making sure he had the time to get his smile fixed. While Bruce continued to regularly attend the New Hope meeting along with a variety of others, the Atlas office became an informal NA meeting spot as people in recovery brought their cars to be fixed.

Bruce took in everything he could, not just about the ways in which an addict comes to depend on a Higher Power to stay clean and lead a good life, but how the program is structured. He learned, for instance, that the abbreviation GSR did not stand for "gunshot residue, like it did in my police reports," he said, but "general services representative," a person from each group who attends district meetings of NA.

At the car shop, Bruce got a few raises, roughed up a customer who didn't want to pay his bill, and beat a guy who delivered parts. The delivery guy didn't want to bring the parts into the office as was the custom, honking his horn for Bruce to come out and get them. When the guy tried it a second time, words were exchanged, and the man followed Bruce into the office, cursing him.

"I told him he needed to stop talking to me like that, and he stepped in a little closer and said, 'What if I don't?'"

Bruce replied, "I'll take your big ass outside and bang you out."

Which—after getting the green light from Steve and removing his new teeth—White did. Sometime later, Bruce apologized to the parts driver, though his ego still got a kick out of showing the guy who was boss.

After a couple of years at Atlas Auto—making money, saving money, investing some money, and getting a new sponsor to guide him through the rest of the steps—Bruce decided to move on.

(Bruce would make good use of the new sponsor—a man named Majid who lived just four blocks away from him on Maryland Avenue—for the next eight years.)

The time to leave Atlas Auto became clear to Bruce when he witnessed a bit of "nothing personal, just business" at the shop, which troubled a conscience he wasn't even sure he had.

"One day a woman came in looking for a car, she was about nineteen with maybe a two-month-old baby in her arms," said Bruce. "I was busy, and Steve showed her a car with a blown motor. The young lady handed Steve all the money she had and signed a contract for the rest." Witnessing this, Bruce knew his time at Atlas Auto had run its course. He called the woman and said to bring the car back in. He told one of the young mechanics what he had in mind, and the kid was cool with it.

"She brought the car back, and we put another engine in it, and I gave her the lien papers, signed them, and told her she didn't owe us anything and to take care of her baby," said Bruce, who orchestrated the deed without his boss's knowledge.

It wasn't just time to go from the garage; the time had arrived for Bruce to "let go," a Zen-like spiritual principle greatly encouraged by twelve-step recovery. The concept hit home with Bruce early in his sobriety when his apartment on Maryland Avenue was robbed.

"I noticed that I didn't have the desire to seek revenge, that there was nothing I could do about it but let it go," said Bruce, who had no problem in the past shooting up someone's house or car—if necessary, their body—if they owed him money.

"I figured it was God's way of letting me know how much I had hurt other people."

Even with all of the blood, fear, thieving, and death he'd visited on others, it was possible that he had hurt no one more than his parents, the long-suffering Charles and Maxine. He made amends to them at their graves, speaking to them in silence.

"I know they did the best they could," he said. "But it was no shock to me that I couldn't get clean until they were gone."

16

College / Career / Shirt and Tie

"I had never been a good student and did not think of myself as smart."

—*Bruce White*

How many convicts go on to counsel the same judiciary that sent them to prison?

It's a small club, one Bruce White joined after leaving his job at Atlas Auto.

"I went from cursing at prosecutors and judges to campaigning for them—laughing and joking with them at retirement parties," said Bruce, who for a time dated a judge in the improbable second half of his life.

All the energy Bruce had put into lying, cheating, and stealing to stay high since early adolescence was now channeled into recovery and its fruits.

After two years at Steve Sturgis's garage and car lot—where his honesty sharpened as his recovery deepened—Bruce enrolled in night classes at Baltimore City Community College at the age of forty-eight. Though he'd be forever grateful to Sturgis for the good turn his old friend had done him, he knew that God had not saved his life just so he could sell used cars.

FIGURE 16
Bruce White at his One Promise treatment center on a typical day at work. "The young people in my classes would study for an hour," said Bruce. "I studied for three hours." Photo by Jennifer Bishop.

Well into his middle age, Bruce now cared about things that had never meant anything to him before.

"The young people in my classes would study for an hour. I studied for three hours," said Bruce, who wasn't sure that he had the intelligence to succeed.

Three years later in 2011 at age fifty-one—with a grade-point average of 3.66 and research into Jungian theory and Rogerian rhetoric—he proved himself wrong. Bruce earned an associate degree in human services, studies that dovetailed nicely with the idea that the life he had all but destroyed could be of use to others.

"I wanted to help all those motherfuckers out there that were the way I used to be," said Bruce, noting that before returning to school in middle age he had never followed through on anything positive.

He invited his daughter Nikki to his graduation, speaking to her by phone while driving to the ceremony, and she assured him she would be there. She didn't show.

The pieces of a new life began coming together shortly before Bruce enrolled in college when he met a man named Craig Lippens at an NA meeting in a suburb of Baltimore called Pikesville. By this time, Bruce owned two recovery houses, one at 7505 Belair Road for women and a second on Raspe Avenue in Northeast Baltimore for men.

"That relationship would be life-changing for me," said Bruce of his encounter with Lippens. "When I started school, Craig would mentor me on which classes to take and what I needed to focus on."

Said Lippens, "He did it with me kicking him in the ass to do it. I rode him about his spelling and grammar, sending back his emails with corrections."

Lippens, whose family once owned a banquet hall in Northeast Baltimore, was working for Gaudenzia, a major provider of drug and alcohol treatment in Maryland, Pennsylvania, and Delaware. At the time, Gaudenzia had an opening for a court liaison.

"Craig knew I had personality, and I knew a few lawyers and judges," said Bruce. "I liked the title of court liaison. Something about it seemed to fit me."

Who's the Ex-con?

Lippens cracked the door open for White into the sprawling industry of drug and alcohol treatment, and once it was open, Bruce walked in, having found his calling.

But first, Lippens said, a résumé was needed. Bruce replied that outside of lying, cheating, and stealing, there wasn't much in the way of gainful employment to recommend him. Filing his taxes for the first time in his life, Bruce received a letter from the Social Security Administration declaring that his legitimate lifetime earnings came to about $3,500.

"Considering my past. I thought it was a crazy idea," said Bruce of going for a professional job in the straight world. "But there was something about it I liked."

Lippens told him to write up whatever he'd been doing since getting out of prison, and he would take it from there.

"When Bruce showed up for his interview, he was wearing a really sad-looking suit. The other guy who wanted the job was wearing Brooks Brothers," said Lippens, who left Gaudenzia in 2016 for another treatment provider based in Maryland. "I was friends with both of them and wanted to see how they'd approach the interview.

"The first guy started off asking about salary, benefits, and paid time off. Managing him would have been a nightmare. Bruce asked what he needed to do and when he needed to do it. He was humble and grateful to even be considered for the job. That got me thinking that this is what recovery is about—gratitude and giving back."

When Bruce left the office, Lippens's assistant turned to him and said, "Who's the ex-con?"

"Right then a light went off," said Lippens. "Judges and lawyers would be asking the same thing. Except they would see that this low-bottom, dangerous thug who they had previously sentenced was wearing a suit and talking about how recovery changed his life."

Not everyone at Gaudenzia was on board with Lippens's bright idea.

"My boss wanted me to change my mind about hiring Bruce, but it only made me more determined to keep him. I knew it would be a wild ride. A couple of times Bruce got too full of himself, and I had to remind him who was in charge, but it was worth it."

As for White's impact on fellow addicts, Lippens observed, "What makes his low bottom unique is that the losses he's endured—his wife, his freedom, part of a leg—have [nurtured] his spirituality.

"He could not have recovered any other way. Bruce uses his history like a shield, a badge of honor, and he's earned it." Also, said Lippens, "Bruce's ability to be selfless is why I consider him a dear friend. It was by seeing his kindness and humility that I came to see him as trustworthy. That made me think he would be a good court liaison. He likes to pretend sometimes that he isn't smart, but it's the smartest people who know their boundaries."

Which is not to say it was—or is—always easy to be around the guy.

"No matter how you dress him up, he's still the ruffian from Lutherville," said Lippens. "He will get right up close to people and use his height to intimidate them, especially when he does this thing he calls 'the big yard tap'—a sharp, backhand *thump* to someone's chest to see how they react. And he uses jail terms and expressions when he's uncomfortable. It could be a powerful tool if he had a better idea of when to use it and when he shouldn't."

Yet, said Lippens, "The universe put him in my life, and he's been a great addition to it. I love the big idiot."

Headquartered in Norristown, Pennsylvania, Gaudenzia was looking for someone in the Maryland courts system who knew the streets as well or better than the judicial system, someone who could speak with insight and candor about addicts about to be sentenced by not-so-street-savvy judges.

The treatment industry is rife with "patient brokering"—a scam known as "junkie hunting," where a tout pays addicts with cash or drugs to enter an unscrupulous treatment facility. The rehab then pays the tout a kickback.

While courthouses provide great opportunity for treatment facilities—and Bruce proved to be very good at marketing treatment in the halls of justice—he bristles at the phrase "fishing" for clients. Often, that's exactly what it is.

As part of his tryout, Bruce toured the Towson courthouse for a refresher on how the game is played, accompanied by a Gaudenzia employee who knew the ropes. The first thing that let Bruce know he was on the other side of the looking glass was when a sheriff's deputy allowed him into the courthouse without going through metal detectors. For an ex-convict, it was a moment of self-esteem.

"We walked up the hall where lawyers were talking to their clients," said Bruce, noting that when the Gaudenzia rep introduced him to the attorneys he would "shake their hands and try to remember their names."

On the rounds, he met people in the Baltimore County Substance Abuse Office and began bumping into people he knew and admired from the rooms of NA, addicts who had turned their lives around and now held positions of respect.

"I was beginning to understand what I needed to do for the job," he said.

When they came to Courtroom No. 3, a "jail docket" was in process—a review of cases where the defendant is unable to make bail. Bruce sat down just to see what might happen, a pastime well-known to journalists and, in times past, old folks and idlers looking for free entertainment.

And who happened to be presiding? Judge Robert J. Steinberg, the former defense attorney who had a long and sad history with Bruce White and his family.

"Bobby Steinberg looked up and smiled at me and continued with the case in front of him," said Bruce. "When that was over, he introduced me. He told the court how proud he was of me and how I was an old friend of his and client."

The judge, said Bruce, went on like this for about five minutes. "It was a little embarrassing, and I wasn't sure why he'd done it in such a public manner." Steinberg later explained that before him he saw a Bruce who'd become "the man his father always hoped he would be. I was incredibly proud of him. What a wonderful redemption."

The rep from Gaudenzia had never seen anything like it and told Bruce that if it were up to him, he'd get the job. In August 2009, after a final interview at corporate offices in Norristown, he did.

And so began the next chapter of an improbable life.

The position paid $31,000 with benefits (Lippens fired Bruce's predecessor for trying to borrow money from attorneys at the courthouse), and White immediately went out and bought dress shirts, sport coats, and a dozen ties. He also purchased two pairs of Rockport dress shoes—one in black and one brown, with custom soles for his right foot.

Bruce laid out his clothes for the next day, went to bed early, and the next morning was on time for a job that gave him the privilege of expressing honest opinions about whether jail or drug treatment would best serve a defendant and the public.

If anyone knew all the tricks up the long sleeves a junkie wears to hide the needle marks—all the bullshit employed to avoid a true reckoning with self—it was Bruce White.

"I can help an attorney get a deal for their clients that might not happen without me," he said. "Especially if [the defendant] hasn't hurt anyone."

Sometimes, he testified that the person before the court wasn't ready for treatment and needed to figure out his or her problems behind bars. Sometimes the addict would choose prison over treatment. Now and then—and far from usual—someone gets clean and sober.

"The judges know I'm the real deal," said Bruce, who more than once listened with amusement, disdain, and sadness when an addict's first question about rehab was whether or not the food was good. "Judges who won't budge on treatment issues will listen to me."

Gaudenzia was also looking for revenue. According to Bruce, the company hadn't had a twenty-eight-day client covered by insurance for about a year when he came on board. As well, he said, the weekend inpatient program was struggling, and there were only about a half-dozen in the outpatient program in the Baltimore County suburb of Owings Mills.

"I was told that if I was able to help any of these programs, I'd be doing my job," said Bruce, who soon landed his first paying, twenty-eight-day client on a referral from an attorney in recovery who'd been a childhood friend.

"I made the arrangements for the man's admission and felt like I could do this job well," said Bruce, who began to aggressively market Gaudenzia in all the county courthouses, including the Circuit Court in Towson where he had received his prison sentence for aiming a gun at a police officer.

Amends from a Monster

One afternoon, Bruce was representing a client at the Walker Avenue courthouse in the suburb of Catonsville and had some time to kill. That was the day he came face to face with the architect of the slam-dunk case against him—prosecutor Jill Pickett, who had married and was now Jill Savage.

Aside from the SWAT team that he believes lied about identifying themselves before shooting him in 1998, there was perhaps no one Bruce would have liked to take revenge against more than Savage, the woman upon whom he unleashed a load of venom at his sentencing a decade earlier.

But this was 2009, and Bruce was a few years into righting the sinking ship that had been his life. Now that he was working in various Baltimore area courthouses for Gaudenzia, Bruce would see Savage now and again, vaguely recognizing her but never quite sure.

"I'd been nodding politely to her in the hall for a few months. I didn't know her name and never saw her try a case," said Bruce. "That day, I was walking around talking to people, seeing if anybody needed me."

In one courtroom stood the woman to whom Bruce had been nodding hello. She was talking to a colleague, someone Bruce was friendly with. When White walked over to say hello, he heard the woman's voice.

"It sounded familiar," he said. "But I couldn't place it."

And then it dawned on him—it was *her*—the small but tough prosecutor who had successfully argued the weapons and assault case against him that took a jury less than half an hour to decide.

The realization so unsettled Bruce he had to walk into the hall and take a moment.

"I had a million emotions going through my head," he remembered, having by this time worked his way through all twelve steps of the NA program, which include making amends for past wrongs.

"I had never added her to the list of people I needed to make amends to, so I sat down quietly and prayed for guidance."

Then he got up, paced the hallway, and waited for Savage to come out of the courtroom where she'd been talking with a fellow prosecutor.

"I saw her coming out," he said. "She opened the door and was about fifteen feet from me. As she was getting ready to walk off, I asked if I could have a minute of her time. She smiled and said yes and kept looking at me."

What Savage saw was a middle-aged man in a suit and tie with graying, close-cropped hair and lines on his face from traveling forty years of hard road. Bruce began by saying that he owed her an apology. When the comment didn't register, he reminded Savage of his case, noting that after he was sentenced, "I said some things to you that I shouldn't have."

To which Savage, a tough cookie in her own right, blurted out, "You're Bruce White?!" And took a few steps back.

Bruce told her about his recovery from addiction and the change it had made in his life; that he was "truly sorry" for the way he had treated her. Savage replied that she was happy he was doing well and told him to keep it up. Then she turned and walked away.

Two years later, in 2011, Bruce graduated from community college and gave a picture of himself at the ceremony to Savage, who had once called White the most frightening defendant she had ever put away. For a time she kept it in on her desk at work as a reminder that in the world of crime and punishment, you just never know.

> "The low-bottom addict, the one who's lost
> everything—motherfuckers like me, that's the guy
> I want to help, and I don't want to turn any of them
> down."
>
> —*Bruce White, treatment provider*

After several years as a "trainee" drug counselor at Gaudenzia, Bruce passed the Certified Supervised Counselor for Alcohol and Drugs test administered by the State of Maryland.

And then, after six years with the facility—making about $37,000 by 2015 without enough accolades to suit him—he decided to go it alone in a crowded industry. Those years were a crucial apprenticeship for the "One Promise" treatment business he established in Northeast Baltimore in 2016. The facility in the 6700 block of Belair Road was licensed that July and began treating clients in November.

He named the company after the "One Promise" described in the basic text of Narcotics Anonymous: "An addict—any addict—can stop using drugs, lose the desire to use, and find a new way to live."

There is big money in the business of helping addicts, and each referral tends to bring in revenue. Bruce said that he pays himself a salary in the low six figures as the founding president of One Promise, drives a luxury automobile, and is fond of fine clothes and jewelry. This, said White's mentor Craig Lippens, creates resentment in some of his competitors.

"There are a lot of shady people in this field," said Lippens. "Bruce is the opposite of that."

Bruce began with "quarter-way" houses that provided housing for addicts who submitted to random drug testing. He then built it into a full-scale treatment facility, outsourcing detoxification and offering classes for DWI offenders that are often part of mandatory sentencing for those convicted of drunk and impaired driving.

"We keep beds available for the indigent who have nothing. I will not refuse treatment solely because of finances," said Bruce. "My policy is that kindness comes first—with firm boundaries."

After one random testing for drugs at a recovery house, nine residents—including the manager—were made to leave.

If Bruce learned nothing else from his own story, it's that nothing works until the addict is ready. And even then there is no guarantee. Remember the doubts of the earnest judge who released Paul Geshelin to a series of rehabs that failed?

"I hope I'm doing the right thing," said James W. Murphy in turning the addict doctor over to treatment.

The twenty-year-old Bruce White who shot dope with Geshelin would have argued that the doctor should not have been charged at all. The sixty-one-year-old, seventeen-year clean and sober Bruce might well have told the court that only jail could help a liar, cheat, and thief such as he himself was once upon a time.

Through his work with Gaudenzia, Bruce came to understand that the job of providing treatment "was a product of my recovery, but it wasn't my recovery."

"One Promise"—a headquarters and eight residential recovery houses driven by abstinence-based care—is one of the busier drug treatment and counseling centers in Baltimore. In late 2020, it fluctuated between twenty-three and twenty-five employees with an annual payroll of $1.2 million, according to White, allowing him to provide beds for ninety addicts. Bruce sees himself in every one.

"I get calls from people in jail," he said. "They say, 'Mr. Bruce, can you help me?'"

This is likely the ninth life of a strange and resilient cat whose most recent motorcycle accident was July 2016. In his "slow walk back" to sanity, Bruce White says he "finally found my calling."

And is running with it.

"If we could go back to high school and tell people what Bruce is doing now . . . ," said Joe Bien. "They would laugh and laugh and laugh."

17

One Promise

"An addict—any addict—can stop using drugs, lose
the desire to use, and find a new way to live."
                        —*the only "promise" in the basic text
                        of Narcotics Anonymous*

It's not a dilemma most entrepreneurs face: begin selling high-end used cars or open a shelter for vulnerable women struggling to overcome drug addiction and life on the street.

That's the choice that vexed Bruce White as the 2008 Labor Day weekend neared. He was three years out of prison, five years past his last shot of dope, anchored in recovery, and restless.

"I was barely surviving, and I hated selling cars," said Bruce, who had been supporting himself in the used-vehicle trade for a year and would do so for about two more. The lack of safe havens for female addicts was brought to his attention at an NA meeting. The answer revealed itself the next day in his morning meditation.

At the meeting in late August, a young woman had approached Bruce after the final prayer and asked if she might speak to him, addressing him as "Mr. Bruce." White didn't really know her but said yes, of course she could.

"She told me she was living in a recovery house and she couldn't pay her rent. The guy who owned the house went into her room and said she could [perform fellatio] for the rent—that if she used to do it for drugs she could do it" for a place to sleep.

Homelessness her only option, the woman complied.

"She asked me if I knew of anywhere safe where she could live," he said, noting that a combination of his street cred and a growing respect for his recovery had prompted a few people to come to him with problems. "I apologized and said I did not."

The woman's predicament vexed Bruce. "Even with everything I'd done in my life, I knew this was terribly wrong," he said. He was disturbed enough to bring the situation into his morning meditation the next day and several days after.

At the time, the guy he'd been selling cars with, an Iranian-born national named John, who identified as Persian, owned an old motel at 7505 Belair Road, about a mile north of the "Car City" lot where Bruce also moved autos. John wanted Bruce to take the place over. Bruce also ran a livery service, with a dozen sedans on the road.

"He asked me what I could do with the building, if I wanted to do a high-end car lot there," said Bruce. "I had no idea."

All of which rattled in Bruce's mind as he tried to calm his thoughts in meditation and prayer: a two-story, defunct motel along a seen-better-days stretch of urban highway and a young woman being told that if she wanted shelter from the storm she'd have to trade sex for it.

From it emerged an idea that became the "Hen House," the nickname for the first recovery residence launched by Bruce White—thirteen beds for women, and one for a female house manager, a safe place for addicts to get clean and start over.

FIGURE 17
Bruce White outside the One Promise treatment and counseling center in Northeast Baltimore. Photo by Jennifer Bishop.

The first manager was a recovering addict with auburn hair and, said Bruce, "positive energy," named Heather M. The sobriquet "Hen House" was made in jest by another woman and took hold.

The name Heather herself bestowed on Bruce's fledgling enterprise is anything but a joke: One Promise.

The Hen House began with free, used furniture that Bruce and a friend picked up around the state in a borrowed truck. The project struggled at first, not unlike the people who would live there, but in about six months it began to run at capacity and support itself.

"It seems," said Bruce, looking back, "that God had a plan for 7505 Belair Road that I did not know about."

The house accepted its first client on January 25, 2009. In NA's Daily Reflections calendar of spiritual maxims, a phrase is written

on that date and recalled often by Bruce: "I will find joy in witnessing the recovery of another."

The old, 1950s-era "traveler's lodge," said Bruce, "was my first
recovery house, and it gave me the privilege of being the first man
that many of these women ever knew who only wanted the best
for them."

It remains in operation more than a decade later, and, White
noted, "hundreds of women have come through, and many have
done very well."

One resident, among the second or third group there, celebrated
eleven years clean in 2020 and earned a master's degree. Bruce
isn't sure what became of the woman who approached him nearly
a dozen years ago, desperate for a safe place to live. Like the
nodding-off addict who gave him his first Narcotics Anonymous
directory in 2005, she was, he said, "a messenger."

Bruce took to the business of sheltering addicts like a savvy kid
playing Monopoly. The beds he maintains for addicts are spread
over seven facilities—four owned, three leased—through two
businesses with the name "One Promise."

The first are his "transitional" houses (commonly known as half-
way houses), an LLC corporation. "One Promise Counseling and
DUI" is established as an S-Corp.

"I never had the belief that I could make an honest living, let
alone [enjoy] abundance," said Bruce of the business launched
from a derelict motel on a used-car lot.

"People ask me if I own One Promise," said Bruce. "I tell them
I'm just the guy who keeps the floors clean."

People ask him all sorts of things, especially by phone in the wee
hours, always some variation of "help."

"They call and I hear their shaky voice. They never have a pencil
ready to write the number down. I can usually tell if they're high

or in withdrawal. My first instinct is to be judgmental, but then I remember the way I used to be."

During lunch at a downtown diner, as Bruce talked about his fervent wish that his daughter will get clean and stay clean—hope dashed and renewed, dashed and renewed, seemingly inexhaustibly—the phone rings. He sets down his soup spoon and takes the call.

"Bruce White, how can I help you? Oh, hi, Shaniqua. How are you doing, darling? Who is your warrant with? I will call the judge for you."

Another call on another day, Bruce speaking to the relative of an addict who wants to believe that her loved one is ready, once again, for treatment. "All I can tell you," said Bruce, "is that he walked out the last time we helped him."

He no longer answers the 6 a.m. call—be it on his work or private number—because at that hour, he said, a junkie has been up using all night and is only calling because they're out of money.

"God sends me the worst cases, people just like me," said Bruce. "I had a high tolerance for physical and emotional pain. I'd spit in your face and say, 'Fuck you.' Today I pray for people with high pain thresholds."

At one point, while wheeling and dealing with a married couple who viewed the recovery industry as a cash cow and bailed when the return didn't meet expectations, Bruce leased or owned ten different recovery houses. Through trial and error, on his own after the speculators walked away, White learned how much he could handle, closing some houses and consolidating others.

In June 2009, about six months after the "Hen House" opened, Bruce started an eleven-bed property for men in a rented building at 4204 Raspe Avenue in the Hamilton neighborhood of Northeast Baltimore, just around the corner from One Promise on Belair Road. The house was memorable for being in sight of Epiphany Lutheran Church, from which the words "GOD IS LOVE" shine large and bright 365 nights a year. It was also key to the future of One Promise, because it was here that Bruce began to admire a once-struggling young man who became his right hand in the day-to-day business of second, third, and fourth chances at recovery.

His name is Jason Benwell, director of housing for One Promise Transitional Housing, and clean and sober since 2007.

"Jason was a long-haired hippie kind of guy who didn't like wearing shoes," said Bruce, who in 2014 stood as godfather to Jason's daughter Gia.

(In the same year that Gia was baptized, Bruce was finally cured of hepatitis C—a liver disease contracted by many IV drug addicts—by a drug called Solvid. Previously he'd had more than two years of interferon treatment for the problem without success. The cirrhosis damage remains.)

In a moment that might say more about his recovery than the number of years clean he has accumulated, Bruce was tickled to buy Gia "a beautiful pink dress" while on vacation in Cartagena, Colombia.

Things began to turn around for Benwell a dozen years ago, after his last relapse. When he returned to one of Bruce's recovery houses, White noticed something different in the younger man.

"He came back with the gift of desire," said Bruce. "I spent about a year watching him from afar and saw how much he concentrated on recovery and doing what needed to be done to stay clean."

Which would come in handy for the both of them one night in 2010 after things on Raspe went—predictably given the nature of the business—sideways.

Regular house meetings on Raspe took place on Sunday night. After the meeting—where everyone seemed to be doing well— Bruce received a tip that the house manager and "half of the house" were using narcotics. The rules at all his facilities, said White, are uniform and simple: residents have to attend at least one twelve-step meeting every day; they must abide by their treatment plan, which includes twice-a-week random urine testing; and everyone has to do basic housekeeping chores while respecting house curfew.

After getting word that residents at Raspe were using, Bruce "went home to get a bunch of piss tests" and headed back.

It was a little after 10 p.m. when he showed up, walked in, and surprised the men living there. John, the house manager, greeted Bruce warmly until he saw the drug tests Bruce had brought, and then, said White, "his body language changed.

"I told him I was going to piss the whole house, and he said that I should, that some of the guys were acting sketchy," remembered Bruce, who said the guys who were watching TV voluntarily got up and stood by the bathroom.

"John started to walk away, and I told him I was starting with him." John balked—arguing about how much he had done to keep the house in operation—and Bruce repeated himself: take the test or leave. John began packing.

When the peeing was done, only four of the thirteen residents of Raspe Avenue were allowed to remain, and White's reputation as a "no nonsense" provider of housing for addicts was cemented.

"I love my clients enough to hold them absolutely accountable for their actions," Bruce said.

After this accounting he needed a new house manager, and Jason stepped in. When Bruce closed the Raspe property in 2015, Jason moved up the ladder.

"I offered him maybe $250 or $300 a week," plus lodging, to begin learning virtually all aspects of the business, said Bruce. "It was the start of something we both felt but neither of us could see."

Benwell began finding clients and funding sources to subsidize the cost of housing addicts. He was responsible for maintenance at the various properties and started dealing with Baltimore City bureaucracy in regard to permits, zoning, and the fire department. He remains responsible for paying utility bills at the recovery houses and hires contractors for maintenance.

"Jason deals with incoming clients, helps secure funding and figure out if they have insurance," said White. "He helps get them to detox before they go to the next phase of treatment. He's like a son to me."

In 2015, after shutting down Raspe Avenue, Bruce bought a house at Bayonne Avenue and Harford Road to house men. When old wiring caused a dead-of-winter fire in 2017, he sold Bayonne as is—heavily damaged—and moved on.

The year 2015 was a big one for Bruce. He became a certified drug and alcohol counselor after passing the test for the State of Maryland. He was still working as a court liaison for Gaudenzia and began counseling on the side. For about eight months he freelanced as a counselor at a drug and alcohol treatment center in a Baltimore suburb with a focus on the facility's DUI program. And then he devoted himself to opening his own outpatient facility while buying a new house for women in 2016—seven beds—at 6707 Youngstown Avenue, also in Northeast Baltimore, the part of the city where his work is concentrated.

(That same year, Bruce was involved in the first serious motorcycle crash since the 1984 crash that took the life of his wife and unborn child. He was coming home from a Baltimore NA meeting when a minivan turned in front of him. Bruce flipped over the van and landed on his head and back. White said the driver did not come to his aid, but a nearby homeless man—carrying a sign asking for money—tried to help. Since then, his eyes have been very sensitive to light, and he lost some vision in his left eye.)

White's desire to run an outpatient program was driven—for the most part—by a desire to expand his business and serve Baltimore's entrenched population of addicts. But there was also more than a little "I'll show them" motivation behind it.

In this case, "them" was a local treatment provider who, summing up White's capabilities, suggested that Bruce stay in the housing field and leave real treatment to the professionals.

More than once, Bruce was stymied in his years-long desire to open an outpatient center at 6211 Belair Road, a long-ago private home in the middle of a commercial strip. White bought the property in 2011 and first opened it as a recovery house.

"I just didn't have the knowledge to [navigate] the policy and procedures" necessary for state accreditation, he said. He asked people he knew in the outpatient treatment business for guidance but pointed out that it wasn't in their interest to help establish a competitor.

Bruce was close to accepting—more a resignation than spiritual surrender—that he'd be a guy who owned recovery houses without the authority to treat addiction. He'd already gutted a building for outpatient services and was losing money.

And then, just like the night the desperate woman approached him at an NA meeting to ask if he knew of safe shelter for female addicts, Bruce heard something new at a Saint Patrick's Day meeting that made sense to him.

A woman from Pittsburgh named Kathy H. led the meeting. She spoke about the difference (what little difference is *all* the difference) between "surrender"—key in achieving long-term sobriety—and "perseverance," a less frequent topic.

"She talked about how many people surrender because it's the easier spiritual principle when God wants you to persevere," said Bruce.

And a new arrow was added to Bruce's quiver. Perseverance, he decided, is what someone who ought to be dead applies to good purpose in the new life granted them. "I felt like she was talking directly to me," he said. "I made a decision that night to continue moving forward in making One Promise a treatment facility."

He moved forward with renovations to 6211 Belair Road with a vision of how it would look one day, putting his all into it with the same intensity that he once chased oblivion. In July 2016, aided by a key hire Bruce made from the Baltimore County courts drug evaluation team, One Promise was licensed by the State of Maryland to provide drug treatment.

The first group counseling session was held in November 2016, and the following April Bruce hired a full-time director to helm a program anchored in abstinence and the twelve steps of recovery and spirituality.

In 2018, White purchased the building immediately south of One Promise headquarters, a forty-seven-hundred-square-foot building at 6209 Belair Road. When the doors opened in the spring of 2020, the original One Promise building at 6211, renamed "One Promise Behavioral Health," became a mental health center with a psychiatric nurse practitioner on staff. Treatment there will concentrate on "trauma informed care," to address wounds emotional, psychological, and physical that often lead people to find solace in alcohol and drugs.

According to the University at Buffalo's Institute on Trauma and Trauma-Informed Care, the approach "requires a system to make a paradigm shift," from asking "What is wrong with this person?" to "What has happened to this person?"

People like Pete Cimino, a barber who cut Bruce's hair many times—one of many whom Bruce was fond of but could not save. Cimino overdosed in 2016.

"He was coming up [on an anniversary], and I thought, 'He's got it this time,' but I was wrong," said Bruce.

"I wish I knew the fundamental flaw in people and not just their day-to-day troubles," said Bruce, adding that the demons haunting addicts like Pete are why he established an on-site psychological clinic.

The new building houses administrative offices while continuing with substance-abuse counseling and access to outpatient detoxification.

"There are a lot of [facilities] bigger than me," he said, noting that One Promise does not offer "medically assisted" treatment—drugs to treat drug addiction. "They have their place," he said, "but not here."

He believes that One Promise is "the last abstinence-based treatment in Baltimore. The addicts who make it become part of me forever. The ones who choose not to, I pray for and will help again if they make it back."

By 2017, One Promise was spending about $1,000 a month on advertising. But the facility's best PR remains near daily appearances by Bruce White in court when an addict stands in judgment.

The judicial system, where most addicts inevitably wash up if they don't die first, is a primary source of potential clients, as noted earlier. It also provides a less-tangible benefit. A good relationship with judges and prosecutors, said Bruce, helps earn respect for the recovery community, a profoundly stigmatized demographic.

One day, he believes, recovered addicts and alcoholics may co-alesce as a voting bloc on issues paramount to them. Thus em-powered, they would gain more respect and influence in a society that well into 2021 often sees addiction as a moral failing and not a disease.

"People in recovery have to follow that path [of other once-persecuted communities] to be recognized and considered com-plete citizens," said Bruce, whose own status in legitimate society was questioned when he began working with the courts. "Who I had been in the past traveled very quickly," he said. "Some greeted me with reservation. Others were open to finding out if I had changed."

One who was decidedly closed was the late Judge S. Ann Brobst, who years before had successfully prosecuted the 1990 murder case against Cindy Levering, the mother of Bruce's daughter.

When police questioned Bruce about it—wherein a kind soul was killed after allowing a stranger inside his home to use the phone—he told the cops that it was not his style to rob somebody in the company of his ex-girlfriend and her new boyfriend. The story held, and White was not charged.

In 2009, Circuit Court judges for Baltimore County were running for reelection, and one of them was Brobst, named to the bench from the state's attorney's office. Bruce campaigned for the reelec-tion of those judges—Brobst among them—and had residents of his recovery houses pass out leaflets and distribute signs.

After the election, said Bruce, "one of the sheriffs said that [Judge Brobst] wanted me banned from the courthouse. When she couldn't do that, she wanted them to make sure I went through the metal detectors before entering.

"I understood the way Judge Brobst viewed me at first," he said. "She had every right to."

Though he has earned the respect of many in the judicial system, his presence in the courts is still resented by some. Said one longtime court observer, who asked that her name not be used because of judicial guidelines, "There's still a very poor understanding of addiction among judges. There's also the feeling that recovering addicts who are trying to help other addicts are grifters running a different kind of scam than when they were using drugs."

Yet, Bruce and other legitimate treatment providers, the source added, play a valuable, often misunderstood role in a system clogged with cases driven by drug addiction, from shoplifting to prostitution to homicide.

Bruce's professional image makes some people in Baltimore's recovery industry jealous, said Craig Lippens, White's old boss at Gaudenzia who began working with his protégé at One Promise over the summer of 2020 as a program administrator. That image—at once appropriate yet flashy, with his numerous arm and torso tattoos covered by a shirt, tie, and suit jacket, and carried off with White's sense of fashion and a bit of swagger—rubs some folks the wrong way in judicial circles as well.

Having forgone just about everything in his toxic past, Bruce now spoils himself with some of the material fruits of recovery. His expensive watches, however, are no substitute for the Seiko he wore each Friday in honor of his father, an heirloom stolen in the house robbery on Burgess Avenue.

(In 2019, Bruce moved into a new house—much bigger and better appointed than his first—in the suburbs of Harford County, former farmland with a majority white population hit hard by the opioid epidemic of the twenty-first century.)

Those in recovery who don't know Bruce's story that well—especially the good stuff that followed the sobriety he achieved in

2003—are quite surprised when they attend a meeting at which he celebrates another year of being clean.

In June 2019, at his sixteenth anniversary, a woman in the crowd was stunned to see a table of judges, prosecutors, and attorneys there to support Bruce. "Most dope fiends," she said, "don't hang out with judges."

("I have friends in high places and friends in low places," said Bruce. "I love them all equally.)

At first, said the woman—who has been sober longer than Bruce and did not want to be identified—was daunted by the visitors from the judicial world, several of whom she knew from her old life—and held back from saying hello.

"But then I thought, 'What the hell, I'm gonna talk to them— I'm not a criminal anymore.'"

18

The D Train

"The sorrow for the dead is the only sorrow from
which we refuse to be divorced."

—*Washington Irving*

Some 58,000 Americans died during the war in Vietnam,
enough to fill the House that Ruth Built. In the calendar year
2017 alone, 70,237 Americans were reported dead from an overdose of drugs. In 2018, it was about 68,000, the first drop reported
since 1990. The number went back up in 2019 to 70,980, of which
50,042 involved opioids.

Overall, the carnage continued to be higher than deaths from
automobile accidents or gun violence. Against this toll, the name
of an NA meeting Bruce White attends now and again is instruc-
tive: "Grow Up or Die."

The philosophy was on display at the Baltimore County Courthouse in late October 2012 when Bruce tried to persuade a pregnant, heroin-addicted young woman to go into treatment. She
resisted.

"I don't think she appreciated what Bruce was trying to do for
her," said Joshua Insley, her attorney.

In October 2019, a group of women incarcerated at the Baltimore County Detention Center in Towson, not very far from where Bruce attended junior high school, got together to talk about recovery. Much of the discussion was about drugs, the streets, and the decisions that led them to jail or, in some cases, back to jail.

Someone told the story of two former inmates who had attended recovery meetings behind bars, jailhouse friends released the same day, no names mentioned. The first of the newly freed women said she was headed to One Promise to ask for a bed. The other said she was going to her cousin's house.

One of them OD'd and died within days of release. The other was believed to be clean and sober. It was not necessary for the storyteller to specify which was which.

Bruce White can tell story upon story like this, tales that pivot on a deceptively simple choice—do I turn left or right?

From persuading an employee at a methadone clinic to steal inventory and give it to him, to being so fucked up on a batch of homemade MDA at a Genesis concert in Baltimore he believed the laser show was tearing his flesh, the yarns White spins would fill a set of encyclopedias.

And the fattest volume would be *D*, for death. The D train.

"I hear about the OD death of someone I know from my past, or a client or someone I've tried to help, every seven or eight days," said Bruce in 2020. "I couldn't remember all of their names if I had to."

The drug treatment industry—a reflection of the global market for illegal drugs—is a gold mine. And where there is gold, there is greed. Where there is greed, there is lying, cheating, and stealing.

In late December 2017, the *New York Times* began a series of stories on the treatment industry headlined "Addiction Inc."

FIGURE 18
Bruce (*right*) and his brother Woody, circa 2018. "I never thought he would live this long," said Woody. "No one did." Photo courtesy of Macon Street Books.

The subhead of the four-part series read, "Marketing Wizards and Urine-Testing Millionaires: Inside the Lucrative Business of America's Opioid Crisis."

The nation's addiction crisis, the story declared, is the "defining feature of the early 21st century American experience." And then: "In crisis, there is opportunity—and the entrepreneurs have swept in."

They might well have said vultures, according to a "personal history" in an October 2019 issue of the *New Yorker* by self-declared addict Colton Wooten.

According to Wooten, South Florida—an area of dense population that includes the counties of Broward and Miami-Dade, along with the city of Palm Beach—had 478 licensed facilities for drug treatment when his story was published. That, he reported, was more than the number of public elementary schools in the same area.

Addiction, treatment, billing for insurance, relapse, billing for insurance, more treatment, and another relapse is known in the rehab community as "the Florida shuffle," and it represents, the *New Yorker* asserted, "a constant flow of revenue."

As of 2020, in all of Maryland—twenty-four counties and the city of Baltimore, about six million people in all—there were 363 outpatient facilities and 363 "intensive outpatient facilities" (IOP), the category to which One Promise belongs.

White said he must abide by a minimum of four state regulatory agencies, and that while Florida has long been infamous for lax regulation of treatment providers, the negative national press of the past five years has begun to tighten things up.

Though White rarely reads for pleasure, he keeps up with the latest approaches to treatment, which currently include ways to deal with trauma underneath an addict's drug use. As for headlines about unscrupulous providers, he said he doesn't need the media to know two things: that the industry in which he makes a good living is rife with charlatans, and that he is not one of them. "Many people get into this field for the money. That's not my story," he said. "Unethical providers should be dealt with harshly and, in most cases, imprisoned."

He tells of a "business call" a physician accompanied by a licensed clinical professional counselor made to One Promise in late

2019. "They told me how much money I could make if I gave my clients access to Suboxone [a drug that eases opiate withdrawal] and a methadone program," said Bruce. "They said I could make between $300,000 and $800,000 guaranteed a year."

Bruce asked the women if they were aware that his work was inspired by something bigger than money.

"They looked at me like there was something wrong with me. So I asked them if they wanted to know what that 'bigger thing'" was now advising him to do.

They said yes, nearly in unison, and Bruce replied, "It's telling me to get you the fuck out of my office."

To what does he credit his portion of the moral high ground?

"My horrific past," he said.

Bruce has a thick deck of funeral and memorial cards, which, if laid side by side, would make a yearbook of tragedy.

The thin pieces of paper—name, date of birth, date of death, and a few lines of verse designed to comfort—represent a fraction of the addicts Bruce has tried to help who did not make it. He estimates that he has known, either well or peripherally, more than one hundred people who have died from the disease of addiction.

"Selfishness and self-centeredness gets most of them," he observed. "The needle just finishes the job."

The overdose death of One Promise client Nick DeLara on December 10, 2016, disturbed Bruce more than most: "the only one that brought tears to my eyes," he said.

Nick was an expert car detailer from the rough warrens of Monroe Street in Southwest Baltimore. Bruce knew something was wrong when Nick failed to show up back at the house on Louise Avenue where he was a house manager.

DeLara was found dead from an overdose in a Baltimore County motel room.

"I was so mad when I got the news and sad at the same time," said Bruce. "I knew if Nick used again he'd die. I think he knew it too. His pain was so great that nothingness was welcome."

At the twelve-step meeting where Nick was mourned instead of celebrated—attended, Bruce said, by about one hundred people—White saw someone in the crowd who had crossed him in a way that would have resulted in mayhem worthy of the Big Fucking Indian in the old days. The man was someone Bruce had once sponsored in NA, an addict who since then had been identified as the person who'd robbed his house on Burgess Avenue several years before.

It was an opportunity—and perhaps a way to honor the death of an addict who didn't make it—for Bruce to practice one of the keystones of recovery: forgiveness. Yet his first reaction to absolving the thief was "fuck that shit." And then he thought better of it.

"I had Nick in my heart, and I was looking at the young man who had robbed my house after I'd given him my time and trust," said Bruce—who also was aware that he himself had done much worse to friends and family in his own addiction. "He'd never been able to stay clean and was constantly in and out of jail and rehab."

Bruce asked the guy to take a walk with him. Once they were alone, he said, he told the man "to stop carrying the burden of robbing my house, focus on recovery, and move on."

"I'm sorry, Bruce," the man replied.

"I know," Bruce recalled telling him. "Just stop using." (Bruce said the man overdosed and died in 2022.)

Rarely, said White, are active drug addicts impressed—at least not for very long—by the death of a fellow traveler. They mourn, but the shock is seldom enough to prompt them to ask for help. And if they do reach out, they often change their mind or give up.

It makes little difference if the newly dead was someone close—a best friend, sibling, or spouse—or an addict among the rich, famous, and talented. Like Tyler Skaggs.

A major league pitcher with the Los Angeles Angels of Anaheim, the twenty-seven-year-old Skaggs was found dead in early July 2019 in a hotel room north of Dallas. Suicide and foul play were ruled out early, leaving some type of swift disease as a possible cause. Or, as the autopsy found, a drug-related death, one in which Skaggs—knocked out on a combo of booze, fentanyl, oxycodone, and oxymorphone—choked on his vomit, not unlike Jimi Hendrix a half-century earlier.

In October 2020, a veteran Angels employee in the media office—Eric Prescott Kay—was indicted for distributing the fentanyl that Skaggs used before his death.

"I called that the day it happened," said Bruce. Asked if such a high-profile death from addiction has an impact on the people he treats, White replied, "Zero."

"These kids are immune to feeling someone's death," he said, noting that the new breed of addicts—kids forty years younger than Bruce, who came of age in an era where it's virtually impossible to rob a pharmacy with a gun—seem to be wholly without empathy.

"Their ego tells them it won't be them. I have a client that woke up beside his dead girlfriend and another who found her husband dead on the floor in their baby's room. The only way they can continue to use it is to be oblivious and numb to the passing of another addict."

"Oxy" and fentanyl—both synthetic, the latter developed to manage the pain of cancer patients—are the primary substances driving the twenty-first-century opioid epidemic in the United States.

Fentanyl is similar to morphine and up to one hundred times more potent. One or the other—together and in combination with other drugs—have been the cause of most of the deaths in the addict population Bruce deals with in Baltimore.

Ginger Baker, the fabled drummer for the late 1960s band Cream, died at age eighty on October 6, 2019, of various ailments, including heart and lung disease. A notorious junkie, Baker claimed to have quit heroin twenty-nine times. Few addicts in the synthetic opioid era of addiction are afforded 1 percent of those chances, if that.

There are those too who somehow, usually by following simple directions as if their life depended on it, make it to the other side of the street. Riches rarely await them, though now and then that happens. Instead, they find something more valuable and often more scarce than wealth: contentment.

"I see a lot of that too," said Bruce of the exceptions to the rule. While no one knows who will beat the odds, it is the not-too-infrequent triumphs of the spirit that keep White going amid so much waste, heartache, and darkness.

Back when he resided at the Maryland House of Correction in Jessup, he'd see inmates buried out back and think, "'If I die here they're going to have to pay people to carry me to my grave.'"

Charles and Maxine White did not live to see their youngest son become "one of them," the small percentage of hard-core drug addicts who get clean, stay clean, and lead productive lives.

Along with the death of his wife (for which he carries the greatest remorse) and the distance that drugs have put between him and his daughter, the passing of his parents before they could see the man he has become is one of Bruce's deepest regrets.

"My parents were always trying to fix me at any expense to themselves," he said, remembering how his mother once drove him downtown during high school so he could cop dope after he'd bruised his tailbone and told her he needed something to stop the pain.

"They didn't realize they needed to let me hit my own bottom, as painful as that may have been for them."

The monster that was Bruce White survived long enough to hit his bottom in prison *after* giving up narcotics. By the time he stood weeping before Judge Kahl, his journey had accomplished what no one, much less his befuddled parents, could. He was done.

On November 25, 2019, the Monday before Thanksgiving, Bruce White made an appearance before eleven judges in Baltimore County Circuit Court, with Chief Judge Kathleen Gallogly Cox front and center. In front of a courtroom packed with spectators, Bruce sat alone at the defense table in a light gray suit, blue shirt, and tie.

Lining the walls on the left and right sides of the courtroom are portraits of some two dozen judges who had ruled the bench before their deaths. On an easel in front of Bruce was a portrait covered in black velvet. Beneath the shroud was an oil painting of Judge Christian Kahl, the man who in 1998 sentenced White to twenty years in prison.

The event was the unveiling of Kahl's portrait before it joined those on display.

After opening remarks, Bruce was introduced, an honor known by few ex-felons—a distinction, he said, more valuable than a possible pardon.

At Kahl's 2016 funeral, a eulogy mentioned Bruce as a positive result of the jurist's compassion when the judge acted on the change he saw in White in 2005 and released him. Now, Bruce was speaking for himself, a sheaf of papers folded in his left hand, a large fragment of a bullet from the SWAT team shooting still lodged below the elbow.

Never at a loss for words, Bruce was quiet for a moment before speaking in a halting voice. He referenced the sexual trauma of his childhood and how, when Kahl released him, he was no more than a broken and bawling fourteen-year-old in a prison uniform.

"This is a very big deal for me," he said, thanking Judith Lynn Kahl, the judge's widow, for the opportunity. "Even when it was unpopular, Judge Kahl would give people a chance. He gave me that chance."

Going over some key moments of his case—how he deserved every day of his original twenty-year sentence, a man "without a redeemable bone in my body"—Bruce cataloged the unforeseen results of Kahl's mercy.

"Because of his belief in me as a human being, hundreds of people are sober today, taxpaying citizens who are not breaking the law," he said of current and former residents of his recovery houses. Of those, about thirty-five are women who have given birth to healthy babies.

The papers in White's left hand were outlines of a speech he had prepared, several drafts worth, that Bruce didn't find it necessary to consult.

The brothers White—Woody, Andy, and Bruce—each inherited a substantial amount of money upon the 2015 death of their mother's childless sister—Gwendolyn Johnson Hoch. Woody got most of it, and Bruce doesn't really know nor care what his older brother is doing with it.

Bruce was sure that the money would be the death of Andy, whose first shot of heroin he administered when they weren't much more than teenagers. But that hasn't been the case.

At the end of 2019, the sixty-four-year-old recluse was still hanging in there, alone on Thanksgiving Day with a ham-and-cheese sandwich and good wishes for his little brother. Speaking by phone in a near-unintelligible garble and noting that many life-long friends had recently taken their lives, Andy said of Bruce's success, "I'm happy for him."

When the day comes that Bruce fails to cheat death one more time, he will be buried next to his wife Patti at Loudon Park Cemetery in Southwest Baltimore. One Promise, he said, will go into trust.

It is his wish that his legacy include an annual education scholarship for a person who served at least two years in prison and has achieved two years clean and sober. And he avowed that there will always be a bed at One Promise for the addict who has been stripped of everything but the desire to kick dope for good.

As a new decade beckoned, Bruce looked back on who he had once been—"a junkie who couldn't stop shooting dope in his neck"—and said the road from there to here "has been a slow walk back."

And when he does die, he is certain he will not return to the underworld, "where I went when I flat-lined," the place where an old man in long robes, his face hidden from the broken human at his feet, said, "Stop worrying and go on."

Epilogue

A DAY IN HIS BEST LIFE,
THANKSGIVING WEEKEND 2020

And this is how Bruce White maintains the improbable gift to an unlikely suspect that is his clean and sober life.

Be it Thanksgiving Day or just another Thursday, Bruce follows a routine that has served him well from his earliest sobriety. In doing so, he reacts to what happens each day in ways that still surprise him.

Like the Thanksgiving weekend when someone who had come to One Promise for help broke into his office and made off with more than two thousand dollars in rent money from the people learning to be clean and sober in his recovery houses. Most of the residents receive funding from the state. Others, usually those whose funding has run out, pay as they go.

"I wake up around six or six-thirty [without an alarm] and pray and meditate before I get out of bed every day," he said, the day after the robbery. "I use meditations I find on YouTube and say some memorized prayers, like the serenity prayer.

"Then I pray to be of service to others and give gratitude for the life I have. I don't really pray for 'things.'"

His Higher Power, whom he calls God? "A universal energy that is formed in love," he said. "The energy that made the universe that also made you and me."

FIGURE 19
A sitting room at a One Promise residential recovery house on White Avenue in Northeast Baltimore. "Listening to others, considering well what they say, / Pausing, searching, receiving, contemplating."—Walt Whitman. Photo by Jennifer Bishop.

Sometimes his free-form prayers include specific individuals, though not the same ones every day. "And some days it's very personal when someone I know is struggling."

The person at the top of that list as late November of 2020 came to a close was one of a handful of addicts in a group session the Saturday after the holiday. Bruce dropped by his office to get that week's rent money, the part that is paid in cash, a little more than $2,500. His door was unlocked, and the money was gone.

Jason Benwell, Bruce's right hand and the guy who collects the rent and leaves it in the same place every week, had double-checked the door after the drop-off and confirmed that he'd left it locked.

Bruce went downstairs into a group counseling session and announced, "Nobody leave this room"—and then was told that one guy had left just a little while ago and not come back. He had come in Friday night after his mother bailed him out of jail on Wednesday. Bruce had met with the guy briefly, and he had been evaluated.

A check of security cameras showed the man leaving the session, rooting around in the front desk until he found a set of keys, and using them to get into Bruce's office before leaving with the money.

Which immediately led to three things: calling the police, pressing charges, and Bruce including the guy in his prayers.

"I prayed for him to survive, that that amount of cash wouldn't kill him," he said. "That's how you do [gratitude]."

Compassion, however, took a moment.

"I was very pissed off at first," he said, noting that the cash would have paid a lot of bills during difficult pandemic times. "It took me a while to de-escalate. I have the privilege to be the one who is stolen from and not the one doing the stealing. Even without that money, my life is beyond my wildest dreams."

To remain in the place where thinking about others before oneself is a key defense against relapse, Bruce continues to work the twelve steps of Narcotics Anonymous, making another pass at Step One—*We admitted we were powerless over our addiction, that our lives had become unmanageable*—after nineteen years of being clean and sober.

He also takes the advice of his sponsor more than not, attends meetings (many remotely since the arrival of COVID-19 in 2020), and stays in contact with other people whose sobriety he respects.

White also reads and listens to spiritual and recovery literature.

As he has said often, "I am in the recovery business, but the business is not my recovery. My recovery gives me the privilege to have a business that serves the public. I can't mix the two up."

In the evening, before bed, more prayer.

"Just as I've been doing for nineteen years," he said. "No matter what else is going on, prayer and meditation happens."

Drugs and anything else someone uses to dull the pain of being alive have long been identified as the symptom of the disease of addiction, not the malady itself. In Bruce's journey, it seems that love—the kind that skews closer to hard work than the song on the jukebox—might be the last house on the block.

Being loved from afar, the way L. K. from high school "loves who he is" all these years later and many miles away, is one thing. Being comfortable with love up close (where you can more easily be hurt) is the challenge.

"My recovery has nothing to do with drugs anymore, and everything to do with behaviors I don't find flattering about myself," he said. "Turning anger into gratitude, meeting a client where they are in life and not where I want them to be.

"And letting someone love me."

Acknowledgments

I would like to thank Bonni Goldberg, who—on August 11, 1990, in the block of Abell Avenue in Baltimore—told me the truth. And to whatever it is somewhere out there that allowed me to hear it.

Martha Vollmer for conducting several interviews with Bruce while touring his old haunts, and Jennifer Bishop for photographing those journeys through the past. I am grateful to Gerry Shields for our shared love of working-class journalism, and Dean Bartoli Smith, who first saw merit in the manuscript.

And to Bruce, who pushed me—not always gently—to finish the project.

—Rafael Alvarez, Baltimore, Valentine's Day 2022

I am grateful to Jill Savage, the prosecutor who sent me to prison, and the entire Baltimore County State's Attorney's office.

Michael Salconi, a fellow traveler who portrayed Officer Santangelo in *The Wire* and connected me to Alvarez.

Also, Kevin Carr and Harry Green for their legal advice on the project and to Jason Benwell for years of trust and support.

Thanks to the bench of Baltimore County for all their support and guidance.

I am grateful for all that my brother Woody has done for me, and I am forever thankful for my mother and father, may they rest in peace.

And all the men who have sponsored me and to Narcotics Anonymous, without which I would not be here.

—Bruce White, Baltimore, February 2022